Tiny Silver
Sparkles

A Spiritual Journey of
Love and Healing

Tiny Silver Sparkles

A Spiritual Journey of
Love and Healing

by

Donza Doss

Soul Touch
Publishing
Dallas, Texas

Dedicated to the man who has made the most profound impact in my life, my beloved Patrick

Acknowledgements

I want to thank everyone who has been a part of my journey in writing this book. My Irish inspiration, Maire Holmes, who believed in me and gave such positive support when I needed it. You are my muse. To Nancy Engemann, who has been my number one fan, who listened and waited to hear each chapter as I wrote them, and witnessed the unfolding of my story. Kellee Caldwell, my best friend since we were nine. You have been there with me through it all. I love you so much, girlie.

All of my many teachers along the way who have helped me grow and learn on so many levels. Peggy Ann Pratt, you have been such a positive light in my world. I would not be who I am without your profound guidance, love, and support. I will always love you. Sheryl Sterrett, you have been my spiritual teacher and loving friend for so long. I am so blessed. Jan Marszalek, for helping save my life. You're amazing! Joseph Faust, for being one of my best friends and incredible life coaches I've ever had. Dr. Rob Parker, who has helped keep my body, mind, and spirit in alignment with his many gifts for healing. To Michial Joseph, who has been a great source of nurturing to my soul.

My editor and book designer, Brian Moreland, I owe a special debt of gratitude for being such a powerful inspiration and friend. Without him this book would have not been possible.

To Kira Atlas, for editing the second draft of my book. You are such an angel and I appreciate all of your patience and insights. To Deanna Bond, for editing my first draft of my book and for being such an amazing spiritual friend. I love you.

To my dear friend, Elizabeth Marie, who has been a true gift from God. Thank you for painting my book cover and logo. You're such a beautiful, creative soul. I'm so grateful you're in my life. My roommate, Laura Waage, who has been so kind, thoughtful, and there for me when I needed her most. My niece, Jenny Day, who always wanted to read my chapters after I was finished. Thanks to my little sister, Lisa Chapman, who is like my own daughter. My nephew, Geraine Doss, who loves me unconditionally and always believes in me no matter what.

Special thanks to Susan Ellis. Without her love, support, and guidance I would not be here today. You brought me back to life so many times with her brilliant healing abilities. To Patti and Keith Moreland, two incredible friends who are like family to me. I adore you.

Meagan Graham, I am blessed to have your sweet, sensitive soul in my life. Thank you. To my big brother, Charles Doss, who was an incredible writer and encouraged me to write more. I love you. Rest in peace.

Special thanks to Mark Pantak, who has been the most powerful, healing force on my path to healing. He has been my best friend for over twenty years and has been the most incredible facilitator for emotional and spiritual growth. Thank you for loving and supporting me through some of the toughest times. And thank you to my friends who have been there with me through it all.

Contents

Prologue

As my plane flew over California, the anticipation of my arrival was almost more than I could bear. So many thoughts going through my mind . . . Will I still be attracted to him? Will I still feel passion and desire? I thought of all the words spoken leading up to this moment. The emails between us were laced in sexual innuendo, flirtation, and provocative teasing. The excitement was so intense and overwhelming that I wasn't sure how I would respond when I saw him again after all these years.

I arrived in L.A. at 12:45 p.m. on March 5, 2009. I jumped in my blue rent-a-car and was off to see the man who I once thought was the love of my life. Would I feel differently about him? Fifteen years was a long time not to see someone. As I approached his building, my hands trembled. My heart pounded. I felt like I was going to pass out.

"No, get a grip on yourself," I said.

Then doubt started to creep in. *What if he isn't attracted to me? What if he feels no chemistry or passion? No, no . . . stop this kind of thinking. You're going to make yourself sick.*

I looked in my rearview mirror, checked my lipstick, pursed my lips together, took a deep breath, and stepped out of the car. I didn't even think to lock the doors. I was too nervous to remember that small detail.

Patrick lived in Beverly Hills off Wilshire Blvd. in a very exclusive high-rise. As I walked into the building, a pretty blond woman greeted me.

"I'm here to see Patrick," I said.

"One moment please." She dialed the phone.

I was fidgety, wringing my hands over and over again, trying not to look anxious as she talked on the phone. She finally hung up. "He'll be right down."

As I was waiting, I noticed the lobby had tall, open windows surrounding it, and beautiful planted trees along the side. I wanted to reach out to touch them and see if they were fake. I mean, I was in L.A. now, right? I walked toward the windows. The sun shimmered through. You could see the light reflecting off the trees inside. Before I arrived at the window, I heard a voice say, "Hey sexy."

My heart expanded three times its size. Patrick's voice hadn't changed at all: slow, soft, sweet, and oh so sexy. Excitement surged through my entire body, a feeling I hadn't felt in so long. I slowly turned around. There he stood. We both smiled. Patrick looked nervous as well, just more laid back. He wore a black, buttoned-down silk shirt and a pair of blue jeans. He looked taller than I remembered, and had his hair cut in this cute, short-and-spiky style. His hair looked how I used to wear mine twenty years earlier, but he looked more chic. His skin was tan and his face had more wrinkles than I had imagined, yet he was still sexy and sophisticated. He looked into my eyes. My soul lit up the entire room. The sparks and attraction were very much alive. He took me in his arms. Our hearts entwined as we embraced. I could smell his manly, expensive cologne when I nestled my face against his neck.

"You are in trouble," he whispered with a smile. "Big trouble."

2

He held me tight for a long while. My insides felt like they were on fire. The anticipation for this moment was worth the feeling I was having. I wanted to rip his clothes off right here in the lobby in front of God and everyone. I was so happy to be in his arms again. I felt like I was home.

I turned to kiss him and starting moving toward his lips. He pulled me closer to the elevators so the blonde at the desk couldn't see us. I could smell the faint, stale scent of cigarettes on his lips as we started to kiss. I didn't even care. I was a bit surprised that he didn't kiss me fully or as passionately as I desired. Not yet at least. I knew his smoky breath made him self-conscious. For the first time in my life, I didn't mind his smoking. Not at this moment anyway.

This reunion was about reconnecting, seeing if there was potential for rekindling a long lost love.

Yes, there is, I thought.

His initial kiss awakened many fantasies that we had shared over steamy emails and phone conversations. I was still incredibly attracted to Patrick. He kept rubbing my back and running his long, slender fingers through my thick curled hair. It felt so good to finally be touched and touching the man of my dreams. This gave new meaning to the feeling of being alive. He leaned in and starting slowly kissing my neck. I pulled him closer and felt his heart beating a thousand times harder than I had ever felt anyone's before.

I whispered in his ear, "Kiss me. Kiss me." I knew this would be the moment that would take us to a whole new level of passion.

"You are in so much trouble," he whispered with a devious smile. "Do you have any idea how much trouble you're in?"

Still not kissing me!

He grinned. "Let's go eat lunch first, or we will never see the light of day."

I took a deep breath, trying to contain myself and maintain some sense of composure. I gently stepped back, taking hold of his lovely hands. I could still feel the energy pulsing between us as we walked to his car.

"Is sushi all right?" he asked.

"Better than all right."

We jumped into his two-door, black convertible Mercedes. As he drove, we couldn't take our hands off of each other. We felt comfortable around one another. It was like no time had passed at all. Being in Patrick's presence was such a familiar and peaceful feeling. I was intoxicated being close to him, this radiance coming from me. A lightness in my body. A freedom from this world. I was entering into a new place. This place was love. I could feel my heart opening, pouring out this overflowing feeling of unconditional, heartfelt love. Never had my emotions been so out of control. I didn't believe this could happen to me again, that I would revisit an old flame and discover that the fire had not burned out. It was even more intense than before. We were both now available to explore this new world of love and opportunity. This was going to be an adventure of a life time. We both knew it, wanted it, and were both finally ready. The stars were all aligned. Our hearts were opening and merging together. This incredible feeling was right out of a fairy tale. In order for you to understand the depth of my love, I must take you back twenty-two years earlier, when Patrick and I first met.

PART ONE
The Man Who Awakened My Heart

Chapter One

It was Autumn of 1987. I was in my early twenties, still young and innocent, very unconscious and starting out on my spiritual path. I had just finished massage school and was thirsty for knowledge—books, seminars, anything that would promote spiritual and emotional growth. I had heard about a healer coming from California named Patrick. He was going to be leading a weekend seminar and doing private sessions. I had no idea what kind of seminars or work he did. All I knew was when I heard his name something sparked in me and I had to know more.

Patrick had an outstanding reputation. Many people I knew were raving about his amazing intuition and talent. I was intrigued. He was offering a one-night-free introductory class. So a friend and I set off for an evening that would become a life-transforming, heart-stopping, mind-blowing event that even I couldn't predict the outcome. Little did I know, many profound and positive changes were about to occur in my young and inexperienced life.

The intro for the class was being held in a conference room at a local hotel. As we walked outside to stand by the doors, I saw many acquaintances. People were going on and on, talking about Patrick's work and their experiences doing private sessions with him. There was this sense of excitement brewing deep within.

Wow, I wonder what kind of sessions he does that has all these people going on about him.

In my naïve thinking, I thought maybe he would like to do a trade with me while he was here. I was doing transformational massage at the time. Even though I had never met this man, I felt a childlike excitement bubbling up inside when I thought about us exchanging our work with one another. Not really understanding at all what spiritual path or emotional healing I was about to embark upon.

Everyone headed inside the room to find a seat. I decided I should go to the bathroom, so I told my friend to go in and save us a seat. There was a bit of a line in the bathroom. Impatiently, I waited. I didn't want to walk in late and have to track down my friend if Patrick was already starting. I couldn't let myself miss anything either. I hurried as fast as I could, washed my hands, rushed out the door and down the hall back to where he would be speaking.

The room was quiet. I looked around and found my friend in the front row. Not even looking at the front of the room yet, I hung my head as I walked down the aisle toward my friend. As I was about to take my seat, I glanced up. There he was, two feet away, staring into my eyes. I literally could not move. Patrick was the most handsome, physically beautiful man I had ever laid eyes on. My heart jumped up into my throat. I was completely stunned.

We locked eyes and then he smiled. I couldn't respond, couldn't move. I quit breathing, as my heart raced. I had heard people talk of love at first sight, but never in my life had I thought I'd have this experience. The energy, the attraction, the complete feeling of love. So incredible. From the second our eyes met I knew this man and I had some kind of destiny together. Some soul connection I could not explain. I felt like I was the only one in the room, the way he was looking at me. I became hypnotized by those big blue-green eyes. They were penetrating straight to my soul. Magic was happening. Cupid had just sprung his bow and shot an arrow right through my heart.

It seemed like Patrick and I were staring for hours, but all of a sudden my friend gently tugged at my pants and whispered, "Psst, what are you doing? Sit down."

I was jolted back into my body. I quickly sat down without ever losing eye contact with Patrick.

Yes, this feeling is love.

I could barely focus on his words as he introduced himself to the audience. The room was completely full. He had drawn in an amazing group of people, who all looked very curious as to what he had to say. It was hard to pay attention at first, because I was attracted to him. I felt this deep, dynamic surge of sexual energy being awakened inside. I had never felt anything so strong before. It was much more than just lust. I felt I had found "The One!" The man who would be able to pierce through this shield of protection that had guarded my heart for so long. The man who would see through all my many defenses and trust issues. Wrap me up in his gentle, unconditional, loving arms. And help me heal all of those childhood wounds that kept me trapped in a world of dysfunction and fear. I sensed a precious gift was about to be given to me in a way I had never known before.

He started sharing himself, telling us what he did and all the many things that he taught. He was a body language expert, a professional rebirther, seminar leader, and also did private sessions. He could help remove negative thought forms from your body that were creating diseases. He said he was able to do this in a very gentle, non-evasive way so you felt safe. I just smiled for I knew that there was something incredible this man was meant to do in my life. Dallas had no clue who had just arrived and what a profound impact he was going to make for many people in this big

Texas city. I really had no idea myself, but oh, what an impact he was already making on me!

*   *   *

The intro came to a close and I had to introduce myself. I felt very shy and self-conscious. It seemed like he would be able to read my every thought and feeling. I was embarrassed to even talk to him. I remembered something Tony Robbins had said: "If you can't, you must." I walked right up to Patrick. Actually, I was the first one to approach him since I was in the front row and all. I stuck my hand out to shake his, but instead he wrapped his arms around me and hugged me tight. My knees went weak. His hug took my breath away. His smell was one of the sweetest, most intoxicating fragrances I had ever encountered. I was melting right there in his arms, and I'm sure he was able to feel that I was about ready to faint.

I pulled away and said in very fast voice, "Hi, I'm Donza."

"Hello, Donza, I love your name."

"Oh, it's Portuguese and it means dancer." I smiled.

"Do you dance?" he asked.

"Yes, and also teach gymnastics." I gleamed, really trying hard to hide my attraction towards him. I told him I was interested in taking his seminar and doing a private session with him. Then I shared that I was also a massage therapist and asked if he would be interested in doing a trade with me.

"Yes," Patrick replied without hesitation. "Let's talk about it more over the weekend after the seminar."

I was now beaming. The whole weekend with this incredibly sexy, beautiful man, plus a private session! My excitement was almost uncontainable. I looked back and saw that a long line had formed and said good-bye for now. I could still feel his eyes on me as I floated down the aisle toward the door. I looked back one final time to see if I was right, and yes, his eyes were following me right out the door. I stopped and did a little nod to let him know I knew. He lifted his eyebrows up and nodded back. The rush of energy that had just flooded over my body was overwhelming and exhilarating. It felt like the windows of heaven had just opened up and God had sent this spiritually enlightened man down on earth especially for me.

But no heavenly signs prepared me for the journey I was about to take.

Chapter Two

Two days until the seminar. I could hardly wait. The day before the training I received a call from Patrick's coordinator. "He has an opening at one in the afternoon today. Will you be able to take that time?"

"Yes!" I thought we would be doing the private session after the seminar, but I was thrilled to hear that we would be doing it before. I only had a couple of hours before I had to be there. I jumped into the shower, washed my spiky dark hair and got myself ready. I was nervous and filled with anxiety. What was he going to be doing to me in this healing session? I mean, I was this twenty-something-year-old athlete, a body builder, fitness trainer, along with being a massage therapist and gymnastics teacher. What could Patrick possibly do that would have me feel comfortable and relaxed enough to trust him? I couldn't even imagine.

I left early to make sure I wouldn't be late. I was feeling apprehensive about going, but there was no turning back now. I couldn't wait to take one more look at him, be close and smell him. Being in his presence was such a special feeling. All I could hope was that those feelings hadn't faded away. Was it just a passing moment? A one-time phenomenon? So many thoughts were blazing through my mind as I arrived fifteen minutes early.

I waited in the lobby of this rundown office building. *What a strange place to do healing sessions.* This building was cold and drab, not much style at all. So different from this good-looking, California-tanned guy who looked like he could have just stepped out of GQ magazine.

I started to feel uncomfortable that no one had greeted me yet. *Am I in the right building?* I stood up. The door opened to one of the offices, and there Patrick was. Even better looking than I remembered. An older lady was leaving as he asked me to please come in. He closed the door behind us.

There were two offices inside one large room. He brought me into the room that had a massage table. The other had a chiropractic table. The furniture had been pushed against the walls out of the way. There were windows all around. The shades were half-drawn. He turned toward me with his arms stretched, motioning to come and hug him hello. He had a warm, gentle energy and was a bit feminine, I must say.

Oh God, I hope he's not gay. The way he hugged me, I knew he wasn't gay. He wrapped his arms around me like he had known me for years. Normally that would have made me feel uneasy, but with him it felt so natural and welcoming. I noticed he was wearing the same cologne as when we had first met. I loved the way he smelled. Such a turn on. What could I do? This was his work. Did he hug all of the women like this? Or was I just imagining this chemistry between us?

Patrick released me. "Come over here sexy and let's get you on the table."

Now he's flirting for sure. I had to set all my feelings for him aside for now. This was my professional healing session. I lay down on his table completely clothed, face up. He slipped my shoes off and stood at the end of the table, holding my feet. He took a deep breath and closed his eyes and became very quiet.

What the hell is he doing? I wondered. He wasn't massaging, just holding my feet. No movement, completely still, just breathing and keeping his eyes closed. I didn't move. It felt like he stood there forever, but in reality it was only a few minutes. Finally, he opened his eyes and started channeling all this information about me. Personal, deep, intimate information. I hadn't even opened my mouth, but somehow he could see right into me. He started off by telling me how traumatic my birth was.

"Were you a preemie?"

I nodded.

"Did you have the cord around your neck?"

I nodded again in awe. "How do you know all of this?"

He just smiled without revealing his secrets. He told me how many siblings I had and that I was the baby of the family.

"You are totally starting to freak me out," I said.

"How is the brother right above you?"

"What!" I shouted.

"I want you to say, 'All men don't hurt me.'"

"No," I said.

"I want you to say, 'All men don't hurt me,'" he repeated with intensity.

"Why?"

"Because you can't," he replied. This was the brother who had tormented me for years. *How could he have known this? What is he doing to me?*

Patrick sensed that I was becoming uncomfortable and uneasy. He began to rub my feet, not letting go. "It's okay. It's okay."

My heart beat faster. I was starting to become frightened. I had never told anyone about my dysfunctional family or my brother who always picked on me. I sure didn't want to share it with Patrick. I mean, I wanted to jump his bones, not break down and cry in front of him. I wasn't much of a crier in those days anyhow. I was too tough and never wanted to have anyone think I was weak, especially a man I was attracted to. I thought if you showed any emotion you would be considered this feeble, pathetic loser. No way was I going to be expressing any of that nonsense in front of him.

He paused for a moment. "Did I miss anything else about your birth?"

"Well, I was born with a veil over my face. Do you know what that means?"

He raised an eyebrow. "You were born with a veil?"

"Yes, why? What does that mean?"

"You have to stop hiding. You have so many gifts. You can see. You can do what I do."

"What are you talking about?" I was baffled.

"You are very special and have so much to do on this planet. You must stop hiding behind all of this."

"Behind all of what?"

"Please listen." He moved to the side of the table and gently touched my arm. "You have to get out of your own way. It's time to be seen. You, too, are a healer and you're now ready to go to a new level of awareness in healing." He was serious and sincere. He had such a concerned tone in his voice and a very loving touch.

"What do I need to do?" I asked.

"Let go, just let go of control." He then reached down to put his hands on my stomach. I was a complete freak about my stomach. I wouldn't let anyone touch my abs. I was so self-conscious that my reflexes slapped his hands away.

"No, No!" I said. "You don't need to do that!"

"Yes, I do." He smiled.

"But why?"

"This is where you are hiding all of your emotional pain."

Forget it now. He wasn't going to be touching my stomach.

He stood there trying to convince me that he would never hurt me, that I was safe and would be all right. After ten minutes I finally said, "Okay, but only on top of my shirt." I was too shy and uptight. I couldn't relax or think straight.

What is he going to do to me?

He slowly lowered his hands onto my stomach. I could feel the warmth coming out of his palms and going straight into my solar plexus. It actually felt good.

"I want you to say, 'I am a beautiful, sensual woman who deserves love.'"

"Are you crazy? Why?"

"Because you can't," he said calmly.

"No, I can't do it."

"Come on . . ." he persuaded.

"Okay! I'm a beautiful, sensual woman who deserves love!" I said it as fast as I could.

"Now I want you to say it like you mean it."

My face was feeling hot. I must have been turning three shades of red from embarrassment.

"I can't! I can't! Please don't make me say it again," I pleaded.

"Yes, again, say it."

A voice inside my head said, *"If I can't, I must."*

"What is this supposed to be doing for me anyhow?" I asked.

"You don't even get who you are yet, do you?"

"What are you talking about? What do you mean?" At that time I had no idea how low my self-image was and how I really had no self-esteem at all. I knew there was no use saying "no," so I said the statement again. This time slower, clearer, so he could hear every word. It was hard to say those simple words about myself. "I am a beautiful. Sensual. Woman. Who deserves love." All of a sudden he snapped his hands off my stomach fast like he was pulling something out of it. It startled me.

"How do you feel?" he asked.

"Lighter. It felt like something left my body. What did you do?"

"I removed some old negative beliefs that were locked up in there."

"Really?"

He just smiled and asked me to roll over onto my stomach and put my hands behind my back. I did, just going with it. Then he held my hands and climbed up on the table with me. I was so confused. My head was spinning and my heart was fluttering.

What is he going to do to me now?

Patrick had all of his weight pressing down on my hands. He straddled his legs over my back. "How do you feel?"

"I don't like it."

"How do you feel?" he persisted.

"Trapped."

"How do you feel?" he asked with a firm but kind voice.

"Angry!"

He leaned down and softly kissed my right cheek. "Good, feel that way for a moment."

"What are you doing? I can get you off me, you know."

"I know. You're such a toughie." Then he kissed my other cheek. "Now, I want you to say, 'Get off me!'"

"Okay, get off me."

"No! Say it like you mean it."

"Get off me!" I growled.

"No. Say it again and mean it."

"Get off me, please! Get off me!" I shouted it out louder and louder each time.

"Say it again!"

"Get off me! Get off me! Get off my back!"

"Again!"

"Get off my back! Get off my back!" I felt like a volcano ready to erupt. I could hear my voice quivering. I was terrified of what might come spewing out of me. I could feel all of these emotions wanting to come out. All of a sudden I stopped yelling and tears unleashed.

Patrick got off me and I covered my face with my hands. I broke down.

He held me in his arms and kept repeating, "All men don't hurt you. All men won't hurt you."

I cried even harder. I felt like all this toxic waste was dumping out of me. Sounds of pain kept raging from my throat. I couldn't stop crying. He just let me cry in his arms. I felt safe and comforted. Patrick had so much love pouring out of his eyes as I looked up to see his reaction. He wasn't judging me at all. He just held me tight, never once letting me go during my emotional turmoil. He was doing more than just a job here. He was helping to heal the core of my being. He was going inside the pain with me, traveling down, deep into my soul. We were both connected. He kept stroking my head ever so gently. Then he wiped my tears away.

He kept saying, "You're so beautiful. Do you know that? I am so proud of you for having the courage to go there. You are a strong woman. Do you know that?"

I didn't feel strong. I felt like a helpless little baby needing its mother.

He must have picked up on what I was feeling, because he said it again, "You are so strong. You are going to be all right." He was truly the most nurturing man that I had ever met. I had opened my heart up in such a profound and intimate way that even I couldn't believe it was possible to let someone in so deeply and see my childlike emotions erupting all over the place. Patrick didn't run away screaming, nor did it scare him in any way. He remained perfectly present with me during a time when open wounds were bleeding out uncontrollably.

He said, "You are giving me a gift by allowing yourself to trust me and witness this beautiful release and healing that is occurring."

I could see in his eyes he really meant it. At this point we both knew that he wasn't just doing his job. He was letting me into his big, precious heart, as well. I could feel that he truly cared and wanted to protect me and keep me safe. He held me tight until all my pain went away. He helped me release my emotions until there was nothing left in that moment. So much hurt and anger were gone. This was the most profound healing I had ever experienced. He held me close, never hurrying or losing connection, letting me know that we had all the time we needed. It made me trust him even more than before. I began to relax now and fully delved down to the darkest places inside, facing the parts of myself I never wanted anyone to see. I had been cracked wide open and there was no going back.

I felt ashamed for crying and letting him see me cry. He must have felt it because he told me to keep letting go. "That's all you need to do. Let go."

Years and years of pent-up sadness and grief kept draining out of my body. I felt more cleansed and clearer than before. There was a space inside that I had never felt open until now. I was no longer filled with tightness or a feeling of restraint. All the tension was being replaced by this overwhelming feeling of comfort and clarity. I kept wondering if he knew how incredibly rare this was, this miracle that was happening to me. I mean, I had always been the rock. I never allowed myself to feel or express deep, intimate pain to anyone. For some reason, I needed Patrick to know that he was the chosen one, the one who was supposed to be the channel for this beautiful healing that was occurring. As I wiped my swollen red eyes, he handed me a tissue.

I sniffled. "You know, I have never cried in front of a man before. Not ever." I was now cradled in his arms, my head pressing into his shoulder. I could still smell his wonderful cologne, even through my stuffy nose.

He looked down into my eyes and smiled. "You made it. You survived."

The session came to a close and I felt totally vulnerable and completely raw. He sat me up and told me that I was going to be all right.

I wondered how long I had been doing the session. Right as I was thinking this, he said, "You're my last one until later this evening. It's now two-thirty. I'm going to need to eat lunch. Would you like to join me?"

A huge smile opened across my face.

Chapter Three

Patrick didn't have a car, so I drove. I felt self-conscious about my cheap, used rundown car. I apologized for the junky mess my car was in.

He quickly grabbed my hand and said, "Will you just relax? None of this matters."

I began to feel so comfortable and at ease in his presence as we took off toward the restaurant. We decided to go to TGI Friday's. There wasn't a wait since we missed the lunch rush. The hostess led us to our table and we sat down with menus in front of us. I was still feeling a bit overwhelmed with what I had just gone through. He must have picked up on that too, because he asked, "How are you doing?"

"I'm not quite sure. I still don't believe what just happened. I don't know what to do with it all."

"You don't have to do anything. You were amazing."

I found it hard to look at him when he complimented me. I felt embarrassed and self-conscious. I couldn't fully allow it in. He knew it. That's why he kept going on and on, one compliment after another until I finally said, "Stop. I can't take it."

"I know, and you can. You're going to get who you are. We

are going to have a very fun weekend together." My face felt flush. I wanted to feel like I was in some kind of control, but I wasn't in control at all. He knew exactly what to say and what to do to melt down my defenses.

We ordered our food and he sat there staring into my eyes. He kept probing about my life and who I was. He seemed to be genuinely interested in getting to know me. But I had already felt he knew me well enough because of our intense session together and the secrets I had shared. It was my turn to ask a few questions. He said he would tell me more over the weekend and then continued his line of questioning.

Patrick had this way about him that seemed as though he could always get his way. The charm and confidence he spoke with was so endearing that you just wanted to give him anything he asked. He knew he had this effect on me, because he had this slight hint of a smile with each question. There was no way I could say "no" to anything. I felt fortunate to be spending time with him. It was as if I were floating right out of my body.

I answered each of his questions, one by one. Although I felt uneasy and a bit exposed, I knew on some level that this was very helpful to me. For I was the vault, always keeping everything locked up inside. I never talked about myself or any of my dysfunctional past. To be honest, I really loved that he was interested and wanted to know more about my life and that he was paying so much attention to me. He made me feel special and important. His charisma was such a divine inspiration. His energy felt almost tangible. It filled the space and allowed me to express myself in a way that I never knew existed. In those moments a deep healing was taking place. For I felt safe enough to open up and wanted to talk and share myself with him—the parts that I could not, nor would not share before. I had no concept of time while I was sitting there. All I knew was that I did not want these moments to end.

Our food arrived and I thought for sure he would want to eat in a silent space since he had been working all day. But in between each bite he continued with more questions. I felt like I had known him for years with all that I had already shared. I did manage to sneak in a few questions of my own.

We finished our lunch and the waiter dropped off the check. Patrick immediately reached for the bill. Of course, I offered to contribute, but he didn't even respond. I wasn't trying to expect or assume anything, but I knew he would be taking care of it.

We left the restaurant and I drove him back to the old run-down office building for his evening sessions. I was having so many feelings toward him by this time as if a light had been turned on deep inside. I felt so very happy and grateful for this extra time we spent together. I pulled up to the building to drop him off. I leaned over to hug him, but he got out of the car so fast it completely took me by surprise. He walked around to my car door and opened it. He wanted to give me a hug outside of the car and with us both standing up. That meant the world to me. We hugged once again. This time I could feel myself going deeper into his arms. He held me closer, much tighter than before.

The energy between us was incredible. The chemistry and attraction undeniable. I felt him wanting me. We held each other for such a long time. I pulled away, but he kept holding on. With his hands moving gently down my back, I took a deep breath and stood there and enjoyed every single moment with him. Especially the sexy scent of his cologne that made me feel dizzy. With tingles spreading throughout my body, I could feel myself starting to fall in love.

This is crazy, I thought. *How can anyone feel this way so quickly?*

I didn't have any answers. I just knew that this was the first time I had ever felt anything so profound and deep. It was as though electricity was surging through every cell of my body. I had awakened to a whole new level of passion and desire. What my heart felt made me believe even more that there was a God. For only God could have brought this kind of man into my life. One who would be able to have this powerful presence and effect—not only on my heart, but also my soul. I felt a love opening up inside. There was only one thing to do and that was to allow it into my heart completely and fully. I'm not sure I could have stopped it even if I wanted to. The presence of love was too strong. I wasn't sure if I believed in past lives or not, but I sure knew that Patrick was familiar, and the fact that I trusted him made me feel safe in his arms.

As we stood there for several minutes breathing together, hugging each other, I didn't want to let him go. *Does he feel it too? Or am I living in Fantasy Land?*

Right as my mind questioned these feelings, he leaned in and whispered, "Can you feel that?"

His heart was beating so strong.

"Yes, I can," I whispered back.

"Mmmm," he said with a big sigh. I sensed he was feeling the intensity of our energy just as much as I did. I felt as if I was going to transcend at any given moment now. The thought of him feeling it too was more than I could comprehend. What a perfect ending for my miraculous day of healing.

He kissed my cheek. "I'll see you tomorrow."

We both smiled big and bright at one another. I couldn't be any happier. His smile was going to be etched in my brain for the rest of my life.

Chapter Four

I woke up early Saturday morning, the day of the seminar. I was so excited to spend a whole weekend together, even if he was going to be teaching and doing his work. I was about to learn all the many things he had to share. The thought was nourishing to my soul.

The training was going to be ten to six with a half hour lunch break. I wanted to make sure that I was totally prepared on all levels. I soaked in a long hot bath and did my best to calm my nerves. I was such a wreck not knowing what to expect. I had no idea if the seminar was going to be as emotionally intense as my private session. I was scared of being that open and vulnerable in front of a large group of people. That was something that I was definitely not prepared for. Although I trusted Patrick and knew that he would not allow anything negative to happen to me, it was just the fact that this was all so unknown and unfamiliar. I wasn't one of those laid back, easygoing kind of gals. I was a complete control freak and needed to know exactly what was on the agenda. I always had to make sure that I was in control of everything. I had no clue what kind of seminar I was about to step into. I just knew it was going to be a weekend of a lifetime.

I finished getting ready, ate breakfast, grabbed a notebook and pen, packed some snacks, and was off to spend an entire day with the man I was falling deeply in love with. I wasn't sure how I was going to handle it all. I wasn't used to feeling so many different emotions all at once, especially from a man I barely knew.

I consider myself an open-minded person with so much curiosity and willingness to learn and grow. I had never stepped this far out of my comfort zone. I was taking a big risk, a total leap of faith. I had a lot of trust issues. Actually, I had a lot of issues, period. So for me to even think about parading my personal business or my emotional baggage before the presence of others scared me to death. It was hard enough to do it in front of Patrick, let alone a group of strangers. At least when I was alone with him, I knew he wasn't going to judge me. But at the seminar there were people who lived in my city, people I may run into again.

I started having second thoughts about going, but I had already paid for it, plus there was no way I was going to miss seeing him again. I had given my word and that was a very sacred thing for me. How was I going to be able to get mentally prepared to take that first step into the building? I realized I would have to do it in small increments. So I started breaking it down. Step one: just get in the car and start driving over there. Step two: listen to music on the way to help calm me down. Step three: park the car and collect my purse, which had all my things in it that I needed for the seminar. Step four: get out of the car and start approaching the hotel where the seminar was being held. Sounded easy enough, but for some reason it just wasn't. I made it over there but couldn't get out of the car. I was terrified and almost started to cry. I was completely paralyzed by fear. Going in there was an insurmountable task. I felt nauseous.

I began to pray. "Please, God, I need your help. Please take all this fear away. I need a miracle now."

I opened my eyes and looked out my car window. As God as my witness, I saw Patrick pulling up in a car right next to mine. I couldn't believe it. He was being driven by his coordinator. He turned and looked right at me. My heart stopped. He was smiling and looked so beautiful. There are no words to express how I felt in that moment. I knew God had answered my prayers and a miracle had just occurred. This overwhelming feeling of relief came over my complete being. I immediately lit up.

Patrick opened my car door and asked how was I doing? I was still in shock as we embraced. All of my fears dissipated with his smile. My whole emotional state changed to this giddy teenage girl. I hugged him back, saying that I was doing great now. He looked well-groomed and professional, wearing a black jacket with a blue button-downed shirt. He was such a handsome man, and I was feeling grateful that God had answered my prayers so swiftly.

As we were walking into the hotel, I thought for sure his coordinator could feel our chemistry and attraction. There was no way I could hide my excitement toward Patrick. You could plainly see he was feeling the same towards me, although he was much better at hiding it. We all walked inside and headed toward the training room. There was a crowd waiting outside the seminar doors. The coordinator directed us all to line up at two different tables placed in front of the room. We received name tags and proceeded into the training room to find our seats.

Patrick had dashed off already. He was getting himself mic'd up and geared to go. I was one of the first people to get my name tags so I bolted into the room and made my way to the front row on the right. I made sure that I was as close as to him possible. Within minutes the room was packed. There were over fifty people here for his seminar. I wondered how many had done private sessions with him and how many were feeling as elated to be here with him as I felt. I also couldn't help wonder if many of the women were just as attracted to him as I was. Did he pay this much attention to all of those other ladies? I couldn't stop myself from obsessing about it. I knew what we had shared. It felt so real and so right. The thought that he may have had similar interactions with other women did make me feel uneasy. Right as I was thinking that, Patrick came up behind me, squeezed my shoulder and winked. That was all I needed to put all worried thoughts behind me.

I was sitting in the front row like the prize pupil. I felt like a teacher's pet, I must confess. I was proud that he had just winked at me for I now knew that he didn't behave like that to everyone else. I was special to him. All of my fears and anxieties were replaced with this inner joy, for I now knew that there was potential for us to have more than just a working relationship. There was more that I looked forward to doing with him. Much, much more. The thought of that began to take my mind down a whole other path of possibilities. At that time I was such a young naïve woman, one who had never been in love before.

As I sat there waiting for him to start the day, I caught myself watching every move he made. We were all waiting for Patrick to get the seminar started. I was eager to learn everything I could. Somehow I felt that it would make me feel closer to him if I learned all that he knew. Maybe that too was naïve thinking. I also felt like that I would know him better and more deeply by his sharing his knowledge and many different talents. The training was to help stop self-sabotage and start to live from your authentic self. That was something I really needed to learn at this point in my life.

Patrick finally motioned everyone to take their seats and stood in front of the room. There was this large white board with markers and erasers standing next to him. He started off with the same intro that he had done at his free night lecture. I didn't mind listening to it again. He had this captivating presence as he stood in front of the class. After his introduction, he took a marker and began to draw a house with many rooms and a small little rat. He then told us that the ego was this rat. It wasn't bad and was only seven years old. Then he put different names to each room: financial, family, relationship, health, and spiritual. He proceeded to run the little rat (our ego) in and out of each room with his marker, saying how fast and destructive our ego can be if we don't recognize it. He gave distinctions to all of our different parts, saying when you compare yourself with another that it is the ego controlling you.

Who knew? I had never heard anything like this before.

"How many of you compare yourself in some way to another?" he asked.

Everyone raised their hands.

"You must stop these thoughts and behaviors if you want to succeed. This is how you keep sabotaging your life and relationships." He went on to explain how our thoughts controlled our feelings. So if we will change our thoughts then our feelings will have to change with them. This was all new information to me. For most of us there, it was a different way of thinking.

"How can you change your thoughts?" He looked around the room. "It's simple. You choose to do so. When you notice yourself thinking negative thoughts or thoughts that create a sad, mad, or bad feeling, be willing to look at those thoughts so you can be willing to change them. Are there any questions?"

Several hands went up.

"How do you stop your thoughts?" one man asked.

"You first must realize that *you* control your thoughts. No one else can do this for you. It's learning to break those old patterns that keep you stuck in your negative thinking." He answered each and every question with ease and confidence. He made it seem easy for us to learn how to do what he was saying. Even though there were many of us that were still confused.

"This is the first step we can learn to help stop our self-sabotage. It won't happen overnight and you will have to practice it every day. Like a muscle that needs to be worked out slowly."

I really liked that analogy since I was a body builder and all. This was definitely a new way of thinking.

He continued to explain more about the ego, "Whenever we see something that is familiar, then our ego tells us it is safe. If it is something that is unfamiliar, the ego tries to convince us that whatever it is it will be unsafe. Since this is new information, your ego will do whatever it takes to find a way to place it in your mind and look for a reference so that you can make sure you will be safe."

It was starting to make sense.

"The ego will have you become more and more uncomfortable whenever you are learning new information. Until you can start to understand and make it more familiar—this means to feel more comfortable—the ego doesn't like change and wants you stay in a place of comfort and familiarity."

I could feel how that part of my ego really ran my life. I always needed to feel safe. I wanted things in my life to be a certain and predictable way. Whenever they weren't, my life would feel out of control and my ego would stir up some unnecessary drama. I really had no clue how much the ego ran my life. So when he was teaching all of this information, I felt as if I were a young child craving more knowledge and nourishment. You could feel the energy in the room coming alive. All eyes were on Patrick and we were enthusiastic to learn more.

He began to tell us a story about our feelings, "Whenever we have any emotion that we want to express, then we usually say, 'I am angry' or 'I am sad.' What I want you to do is say, 'I feel angry or I feel sad' because that keeps you in present time. Whenever you use the words 'I feel' you then become responsible for your feelings and you're in the present moment where your feelings are alive."

Now this was a little confusing, I must say. I had never spoken in that way before. You must say "feel" before you put an emotion to it? This was going to be difficult for sure, because I didn't express many of my feelings openly to anyone. So to learn a new way of speaking was going to take a little time and a whole lot of effort. He was very patient as many hands went up. Again he answered everyone's questions. Expressing feelings was a new habit we would have to start incorporating into our everyday lives.

"It takes practice and by the end of the weekend you will all be able to learn and remember how to speak in present-time language."

I sure hoped that I would be able to learn quickly. I didn't want to disappoint him or myself.

* * *

The day was flying by fast. I was learning many different communication tools and concepts that I knew would be helpful in my life. He asked everyone to find a partner. We were to sit face to face with a complete stranger and ask a list of questions. One person was to go first asking each question. The other person would have to answer in present-time language. You had to be honest with yourself and say what you felt. These were personal questions about your childhood.

"If feelings start to come up, just allow them," Patrick said as he roamed the room.

Now I was really starting to feel worried. I didn't want to do this process in front of a stranger. So I decided I would use this time to go to the bathroom. While people got into their groups, I took off. I thought maybe no one would notice I was gone. I stayed in the bathroom for quite some time. One of his assistants came in to find me. I played it off very cool.

"I'll be right there," I said with sheer terror running through my veins. I opened the door to the training room. Patrick was standing in front of my chair, staring straight through me. I nonchalantly walked back to my chair.

As I approached, he leaned in and whispered, "You're going to be all right."

"I really don't want to do this." I could feel myself wanting to break down and cry again. Of course it was going to be a strange man that was going to be my partner.

I thought, *I'll do this, but I'm going to be the one asking the questions and let my partner tell me how he's feeling.*

Patrick stepped in and said to my partner, "Oh, by the way, let her go first." Then he smiled.

I was pissed. "No, really, I don't want to go first."

"I know, but you get to," Patrick said cheerfully.

Oh, how I wanted to run out of that room so fast and never look back. I knew that there was no way that he was going to let me bolt. I sat down and took a deep breath as Patrick strolled around the room, holding a box of Kleenex.

Great. Here we go again. I sat there staring in the eyes of this older gentleman as he asked all these intimate questions about my childhood and family dynamics. We would have to answer by saying "I feel sad" or whatever emotion described our feelings. Even though we were one-on-one, you could still see and hear everything people were saying and expressing. As I started answering in "present-time-feeling language," I could feel my eyes starting to tear up. I didn't want to cry at all.

Patrick came back over. I wouldn't even look at him. I knew I would lose it then, so I just kept answering the questions and allowing the tears to well up in my eyes without ever looking up at him. He knew that I was trying to hold it together. I was doing so well until the gentleman asked one final question, "Who in your family betrayed you the most? How did it make you feel?"

All of my walls that I had so carefully built up started to crumble. I began to shake my head and put my hand across my forehead, for I had many family members who had betrayed me and I was starting to feel the impact of it all. I had never shared this kind of information with anyone. Not even Patrick. Before I could open my mouth, the tears started to stream down my cheeks. I covered my face in my hands and cried. I felt a gentle touch against my back. I smelled that fabulous cologne which would seem to always put a smile on my face.

Patrick kneeled down by my side. "It's all coming up to be healed. Just stay with the process. You are going to get through this."

I wouldn't uncover my face. "I am so embarrassed," I whispered.

"Embarrassment is just aliveness and it's okay to be alive," he whispered back.

I had never heard that before. He always seemed to know the perfect thing to say to calm me down and help me feel more secure. There was so much more emotional baggage that I had inside. This was a seminar healing those blocks that would keep us from self-sabotaging behaviors. I was finally letting go of my many past hurts and deep unhealed wounds.

After several minutes of processing, he told us to switch partners. I was trying to pull myself together so that I could now be the one asking the questions. He gave us a five-minute break. I was so relieved. I wiped my eyes and went to get a tissue. Patrick was still walking around helping others finish up their processing. I felt so much better than before. A weight had been lifted off my heart. I was more in tune with my feelings and doing amazingly well.

After the break, I started asking the same questions to my partner. I really felt now that I had been able to manage my emotional state. I could be more present as I listened and guided my partner through his process. He didn't seem to have as much baggage or emotional turmoil. I thought maybe he wasn't showing it as much as I did. Nevertheless, I was grateful to get it together so that I could help him, and I did.

* * *

After hours had gone by, it was time to take our lunch break. Patrick wanted us to get together with at least four people we didn't know and spend our lunch sharing about the experiences of the day and what we were uncovering and learning about ourselves. I have to be honest, I was in complete overload and didn't want to spend my lunch rehashing any of my personal experiences. So I went up to Patrick as we were all being dismissed and asked him what he was doing for lunch. I really wanted to go with him.

He told me that he had to get with his staff now and for me to have a great lunch. He could plainly see how disappointed I was. I understood that he had to be professional and keep his boundaries clear. He reached over and hugged me good-bye, which took me by surprise. He whispered in my ear, "You did great today. I am so proud of you."

I smiled. "Thanks."

I pulled myself together and joined a group for lunch.

Chapter Five

As we were all returning from lunch, I started to feel anxious again about going back in for round two. I was also feeling extremely fatigued. I was emotionally drained. I wasn't sure how much more I could possibly endure. We all took our seats and waited for Patrick to arrive. It looked like many people felt the same as I did.

As he approached the front of the room, he looked around and said, "So how many of you are ready to go home?"

Almost everyone raised their hands, me included.

"This is about the time where your egos start to lose control. It's going to have you get as distracted as you possibly can. How many of you have headaches or some kind of discomfort going on in your body?"

Over half the room raised their hands, me included again. It was truly amazing how he knew what we all were feeling. I suppose he was used to having this happen often at this point in the training. Patrick's energy was still so bright and enthusiastic. I wondered how he didn't get infected by this heavy, lethargic energy that was spreading through the room like a contagious disease.

He explained, "Once you realize that this tired feeling is your ego's way of resisting the changes, then all the pain, discomfort, and exhaustion that you are experiencing will soon dissipate, and you will be free from all of those negative feelings."

Just by him explaining that bit of information, I had already begun to feel much better. He always seemed to be right about everything. I really liked that about him. He could lift the energy in the whole room to where everyone could feel the positive shift that was taking place throughout the class.

He started writing on his white board again. He put several words up in a row. The first word was "fear." He then gave the acronym for fear: FALSE EVIDENCE APPEARING REAL. The next word was "intimacy": INTO ME YOU SEE. The final word was "polite": PISSED OFF LIGHTLY.

He then began to explain that fear was another way the ego holds us back from succeeding. "If you just remember that this is false evidence appearing real, then you will overcome so much of the patterns you've been stuck in. It's just an illusion. Fear has no power except the power you give it." It made sense.

He continued with the next word. "Intimacy. This is one of my favorites. Think about this. INTO ME YOU SEE. How many of us allow this to happen in our relationships? This is the key to a successful relationship. You must create intimacy by letting another see into you, all that you have not wanted anyone to see. This will heal you on such a deep soul level."

He continued, "The last word is sometimes harder to acknowledge because of our culture. Polite. PISSED OFF LIGHTLY. If you notice, we actually get pissed off when we are acting in a polite manner. This is because the ego is covering up how you really feel when you are being polite. Truth is that we do not want to be impolite. We feel we have to be polite because of our cultural upbringing. This is another way we keep self-sabotaging. This is when you have to learn about being in your authentic self, to say the truth about what you already feel. Be real and true to your own inner self and stop the ego from being inauthentic. Finally, you must live in your highest truth, then you will feel the freedom and be able to escape from all of your ego's false beliefs and addictions."

It was a lot to process and take in. I really loved what he was teaching and I could feel my mind starting to think in a new and healthier way. I was now feeling more energy than before. The whole room was vibrating. You could see that people were really starting to get it. We all wanted to live in our authentic selves. We all wanted to recognize when we were in our ego. I was inspired and more empowered than I ever believed possible. Patrick had such an incredible way of sharing his abilities and gifts with the world. I felt so blessed and grateful that I was fortunate enough to witness and experience his awesome work.

The training was almost over for the day. People were asking some final questions. Patrick still had plenty of energy. It was as if his work recharged him. He answered all the questions and told us what a great job we had done. He thanked us for trusting him and being open to a new way of thinking. We all stood up and clapped for him. His standing ovation lasted several minutes. He was so gracious and humble. I don't think he expected that, but Dallas gave him one big Texas-size thank you.

"I will see you all tomorrow. Get a lot of rest and drink plenty of water."

I thought I had better get up there fast to say good-bye before the line was too long. Many people were already making their way up to say good-bye. I collected my things and waited by my chair to see if he was going to come over my way. Before I even finished getting my stuff, he was standing right in front of me with a line of people starting to follow him. I stepped in front of him. I was feeling so comfortable at this point that I initiated a hug. It was a surprise to him too. I wrapped my arms around his neck. He squeezed me so hard that it almost took my breath away.

"Great job," he whispered in my ear.

"You're amazing," I whispered back.

"Thank you again."

I had to make this brief, so I asked, "When do you want me to work on you for our trade?"

"Let's talk about it tomorrow." He smiled his sweet, sexy, charismatic smile that made my insides feel warm and mushy.

It had been a long and intense day, to say the least. I had opened up more than I had ever imagined. I didn't know what to expect or what major breakthroughs I was going to overcome this weekend. I knew that there was a higher plan and that everything was in divine order. I could feel my spirit becoming more alive and free. Many of my emotional scars were finally starting to heal. Patrick was the catalyst I needed to break out of this hard shell that had me believing I was warm and safe in my little cocoon. That too was just an illusion. I had learned so much the first day. I had shed years and years of old hurts that even the ways that I walked and stood were completely different now. I had more confidence and reassurance in myself. A new *me* was being reborn. And I was starting to like her very much.

Chapter Six

That evening thoughts of Patrick filled my every-waking moment. I was thrilled to have another day with him tomorrow, then going to meet up afterwards for his massage. I wanted there to be more than this healing relationship between us. I just didn't know how it could happen. I was always professional. Now our roles were going to be reversed and he was going to be my client. I knew I would never cross the sexual line in any way in a session, so I kept wondering how I could let him know that I wanted more. I mean, come on, I was pretty sure that we both already knew what we were feeling for one another. I didn't have a clue where I would be working on him. He wasn't even sure himself.

I had just learned several creative visual techniques. One of my friends worked at the Embassy Suites Hotel by the airport. I knew that hotel well. I never really believed in visualization, nor had I practiced it before. I imagined in detail giving Patrick a massage in one of those big, beautiful suites. You know the ones that have the living room and little kitchen in it.

Why not go with the more expensive room in my visualization? He was a classy, successful man from L.A. So only the best for him, right? So that night as I drifted off to sleep I began to allow my imagination to run free. I ran the scenes in my mind just as if I were watching a movie. I saw the hotel, the lobby, and the precise details of the room I wanted to be with him in. I saw us spending time together after our session. He was very impressed by my work too. This all seemed so real as I kept running it through my mind over and over again. Feeling the excitement of how it would really feel. I knew I wanted more with him than just this platonic working relationship. So I began to fantasize what it would be like to kiss him, actually, to have him kiss me. I was entirely too shy to ever make a move on anyone, especially Patrick. The visions that were playing out in my mind were exciting and completely captivating. Even if these techniques and creative visualizations didn't work, I was still going to enjoy every moment of them. As I fell asleep with a peaceful smile, all of these incredible feelings started surging through my body. I knew I was in for one of the most relaxing and deep sleeps that I'd had in such a long time.

* * *

When I woke up the next morning, I was filled with so much energy and enthusiasm. I could hardly wait to spend another day with Patrick. I wasn't nervous about going today. There was no anxiety or fear coming up at all. I felt this strange calmness and aliveness at the same time. My spirit felt happy and free. I could feel the effect of the seminar and the healing taking place deep within my soul. I was looking forward to another day with one of the most incredible healers/teachers I had ever met.

I arrived at the seminar thirty minutes early. Patrick and his facilitator were outside smoking a cigarette. I was shocked that he smoked. I really despised that nasty habit. I was also a fitness trainer and total health nut, so the thought of him smoking was disturbing to me. Because I grew up with many family members smoking around me, it was truly my least favorite addiction. As I approached Patrick and his coordinator, there was a cloud of smoke swirling around their heads. I didn't want to step in this ring of smelly, disgusting smoke. I didn't say anything about it. It wasn't my business and there was nothing I could do. I walked up and stood right next to him. He immediately put out his cigarette and opened his arms to give me a hug. I was thrilled that he put that thing out. As we started to hug, I was surprised that I could not smell anything except his sexy cologne.

"How are you feeling?" he asked.

"Great," I said energetically. "You?"

"Fantastic. We have another incredible day ahead of us. Are you ready for it?"

I was now starting to have a little bit of doubt. His tone of voice implied that it would be more intense than the day before.

"I don't know. Am I ready for this?"

He nodded. "You will do just great."

I was now starting to wonder what all he had entailed for us. He told me to go inside to find a seat and he would be right there.

More people were arriving and many of them seemed to have more energy and looked happier than the day before. It was because we were much more comfortable and things were feeling more familiar now. It was definitely a lot better than the first day of training. The anticipation of the seminar was now starting to take on a whole new level of excitement and energy of its own.

We all took our seats and again I sat in the front row. I had heard that you retain more information if you're up front. Who was I kidding? I wanted to be as close to Patrick as possible. As he walked up to the front of the room, the audience instantly became quiet. He asked how everyone was doing and if there was anything we wanted to share with the group? Many hands went up. One by one each person shared their experiences about how much they all had released and learned. I chose not to speak. I was not one to talk in front of a large group of people.

Patrick then began to give an outline of what we would be learning for the day. One thing about him was he would always make little jokes. He had a great sense of humor. I couldn't really appreciate it as much the day before, because I had many issues that I was confronting. Today was different, though. I laughed at his jokes. I wasn't feeling as serious or as frightened.

Today, we were going to be breaking up a lot more into groups to learn more about your subconscious mind. Also how your birth trauma affects your life and relationships. I remembered the work we did in our private session. How he knew about the trauma that happened at my birth. I surely hoped this day wouldn't bring those intense emotions up again like before.

Patrick must have known that my mind went somewhere else for a moment, because he walked over and stood in front of me as he continued explaining the plan for the day. I refocused and listened again as I concentrated all my energy on him. He shared about his birth trauma. How intense it was for him. He was born with a cord around his neck, cutting the oxygen from his brain. At that time the doctors didn't know that he wasn't getting enough oxygen and his left brain was not functioning properly. So for years he was only using the right side of his brain, which is your creative, intuitive, emotional side. This made him more sensitive and highly intuitive than most people. It was also very difficult on him, because he knew things without anyone ever telling him. So he could see the truth in most situations. Even if it were a lie, he would know. As a little boy that was very confusing. His mother also wanted a girl. So when he was born his mother yelled out, "Is it a girl?"

The doctors yelled out, "Wrong, it's a boy!" That was the first imprint on his subconscious mind. When he was three years old his little penis began to close up. They had to go in surgically to open it. He said, "Do you see how it was wrong for me to be a boy, and how that was imprinted in my subconscious mind?"

I was mesmerized by his story, hanging onto every word. I wanted to know more, everything about him, actually. I loved listening to his stories. Patrick had such a way of engaging you. I didn't want to do anything except listen to stories about his life all day long.

"Now many of you say that you have no memory about your birth. That's okay. I want you to remember anything your parents told you or anything you may intuitively have felt happened. You are going to get together with a partner and share your memories with them. Notice what comes up for you. Write down how you feel and keep on sharing."

I felt relieved because I knew a lot about my birth. This was going to be an easy exercise.

The lady next to me asked to be my partner. We did everything he told us. It was going very smoothly.

Patrick said, "Whoever is finished can raise their hand." So we raised our hands.

"You two can go first," he said.

"Ugh!" I sighed. "Go first for what?" I started to freak out. My partner and I just stared at each other wondering what we had just volunteered for.

He said, "Five more minutes and I want you all to finish up what you are writing." Then he began to explain that we all have a birth script. "Today we are going to find out what that negative script is and how it has been running your life." Each of us would have a chance to stand up and tell him about our birth and he would help discover each of our negative birth scripts.

He pointed to me. "Donza, you get to go first."

I was completely mortified. How was I going to do this? It was hard enough, one-on-one, but in front of people? No way!

"Stand up," he said.

"I don't want to go first."

"I know, but you get to." He flashed his smile.

Are you kidding me?

Even his charming smile couldn't ease the terror I was feeling. I had never felt so scared and shaky in my life.

He reached out to take my hand and helped me out of my chair.

"Go ahead, Donza. Tell me about your birth."

I think he wanted to use me as an example because he already had information about my birth. I stood up, feeling like I might pass out at any moment. I began telling my story, "I was a preemie when I was born. I had a veil over my face. The cord was also around my neck. I was in an incubator for over a month."

"Great job," he said. "What do you think is your most negative thought about yourself?"

"I'm not good enough."

"The reason you're not good enough is?"

"I don't know."

"It's okay. Say it again."

"The reason I'm not good enough is . . . I'm not worthy."

"Go on . . . The reason you're not worthy . . ."

"I don't deserve it."

"And the reason you don't deserve it is . . ."

"I'm just not enough." I could feel all of these emotions building up inside.

"Say it again."

My eyes started to fill with tears. "I'm just not enough." A single tear rolled down my cheek. I wiped it away quickly.

"Do you see how this is your birth script?" he asked. "You were a preemie. You weren't enough when you were born. You came too early. This is your subconscious imprint that has been affecting your life on so many levels. Can you see this now?" I nodded, trying to hold back my emotions so I wouldn't break down in front of the group.

"You have to realize that you are enough, but these feelings are happening because of your subconscious imprint. Do you understand? This one belief will change your life. Once you understand this fully, you will heal much deeper than before."

I was feeling much better knowing that I may be able to heal those beliefs and imprints.

He said, "The first thing is to become aware of them."

That was exactly what I was doing in front of God and everyone. It felt great to uncover my hidden beliefs and imprints that held me back in every area of my life. I just didn't know how powerful this would be or how much stronger and more confident I would feel after this amazing process. He told everyone to give me a round of applause and he clapped too. "You did an awesome job, Donza."

I was relieved to be finished. I sat down and accepted a tissue.

Each person had a chance to stand up and go through this process. It was the most extraordinary thing to witness. He was able to uncover everyone's hidden negative birth script. It took hours but felt like no time at all. We were all in this process together and I could feel a lot of healing taking place within each and every one of us. It was also very exciting to watch Patrick do his work. It was like magic to see him go to such depth with each person and be able to discover the truth that was hidden deep in their mind. It was as if he were searching for lost treasure. He wouldn't give up his search until he made sure he found all of our subconscious birth scripts (which was the gold). That was my favorite part in the whole seminar. He could take you to a place inside that was impossible to reach on your own, go straight to the core and open you up like a highly trained surgeon, carefully removing the negative and putting you back together with precision and ease. It was such an amazing sight to see, one that changed my life forever.

After he finished up with the last person, it was time to take our lunch break. We were all ready to go at this point. Although the morning had been very intense for most of us, there was still this lightness of energy in the room. Maybe it was because there had been so much clearing or it was because Patrick had a way of changing the energy in a space that would have you feel much better than before. Whatever it was, you could really feel the positive impact taking place.

I decided to go up and ask Patrick if we were still on for this evening for his massage. He was gathering his things and taking off his mic. There were a few people waiting for him as I approached. I wanted to be sure I was the last one to talk to him so I could find out all the details. Finally as the other people left, it was my turn.

"I was wondering where you'll be staying tonight?" I asked.

"I am not sure yet. Do you know any nice hotels by the airport?"

I couldn't believe he was asking me that question. "Yes! The Embassy Suites Hotel is very nice and close to the airport."

"Great, let's plan on that tonight after the seminar. Give me about an hour to get there." He hugged me. "I'm really looking forward to your work."

I just melted right there. I was filled with excitement and overwhelming feelings flowing through my body. He was actually going to be staying at the same hotel I visualized!

Wow, maybe my dreams can come true.

Chapter Seven

We still had the rest of the afternoon to finish the training. I wasn't sure how I could focus on anything else except being with him for the evening. Even if nothing else were to happen between us, I would still get to massage him and be alone in the fabulous hotel I had imagined so vividly in my mind. I couldn't wait for the seminar to be over. We were now off to lunch. During our break, he wanted us to get together again into groups. There was no possible way I could do that. I was sure everyone could see the evidence of my feelings for him across my face. So I decided to sneak off on my own for lunch.

I just daydreamed about our night together, or should I say fantasized? I had this permanent smile etched across my face. I wanted this man badly. I felt so much passion and desire stirring deep within, feelings that had never been turned on like this before. Most of all I was thinking about Patrick and how I was going to be running my hands over his fine, naked body.

How am I going to find the self-control and restraint to get through his session?

After lunch, I arrived back at the hotel for the last three hours. There were a few people waiting outside the doors when I walked up. I was hoping that no one noticed that I wasn't with a group.

I especially didn't want Patrick to find out that I went off by myself. I didn't want to do anything that might offend him or have him think I wasn't respectful of his requests. I was also hoping that these last hours would fly by quickly.

The doors opened and we all went inside to our seats. Patrick was running late, which was very unusual. Finally, he arrived looking even sexier than before. He had taken off his jacket. He had two of his buttons undone which you could see his curly chest hair sticking out. He must have felt very comfortable or was getting too hot. In any case, I was thrilled.

He told us the last hours he was going to teach us about language and how we could stop using certain words that limit us. "There are many words that our subconscious minds do not recognize. The first word we must take out of our vocabulary is 'but.' *But* always negates whatever you're saying before it. Any time you use 'but' there is a negative connotation to it, so instead of using 'but' replace it with the word 'and.' Take the word 'but' completely out of your speaking and you will notice a tremendous difference in your communication." He went on to give us several examples. I didn't realize how often we use that word. It was going to be very difficult to stop this habit.

"Whenever we keep saying 'but' to negate things, it can keep us in a victim-like attitude. We have to be responsible for our communications and the impact it has on others." He walked in front of his white board. "I will come back to the word 'victim' later. The next word is 'don't.' Your subconscious mind does not process negatives. In other words, it drops the words completely out. If I say, 'don't think of a big purple pig,' what did you just do? We all thought of a purple pig. Or if we tell children, 'don't slam the door.' They have to see a subconscious picture of the door slamming. Instead say, 'Close the door quietly.' You change your language to create the outcome you desire."

No one I talked to had ever heard of this before, about our words making this kind of impact in our lives. It was all so fascinating.

He continued, "The same goes for such words as 'can't,' 'not,' and 'won't.' Our subconscious mind does not hear them. They will be dropped out. So we must learn a new way with our words and language in which we find a better and more positive, effective way to communicate. This takes a lot of practice and patience *and* you can do it." He really emphasized on the word 'and' showing us that he made sure he didn't say 'but.' It was really great. I was learning so much and finally losing track of time. I was completely in the present moment.

We then got into groups to practice listening to how people spoke. Each of us told a story to see if we could catch ourselves in our negative language, and then change the way we used our words. This was really a great exercise, because I never noticed or was aware of how often I used the word "but" along with all of the other negative words. This was very helpful.

He told us we had just a short time before we would be finished. He wanted to talk more about being a victim. "If we keep acting as victims then we will be victimized. You must understand that everything happens to us for a reason. All is a lesson we must learn. If we don't learn it, we have the same experience and recurring pain in our lives. We subconsciously create these same events, and they begin to happen to us over and over. If you remain a victim mentally, and if you do not see how you are responsible on some level, then unfortunately you will go through it again. I'm not saying that it's anyone's fault, or you are wrong. I'm saying your soul has created this so you can learn and let go of whatever this is—abuse, a bad relationship, anything where you feel like something was done to you. How can you take your power back if you are playing the victim role? Until you realize that, it is all happening for a purpose. Then, and only then, can you choose to step out of your victim role. Are there any questions?"

Almost every hand in the room went up.

He began to explain in detail so that we all would begin to understand. "Whatever terrible things happened, it was not your fault. We must look at our lives so we make sure it never happens again."

I started to realize how much I played the victim in my life. And because of that, I kept getting victimized. I knew on some soul level I had to go through some of those negative experiences to learn a very important lesson. It was hard to grasp what he was saying at first. Then the more he explained, the easier it became. I was starting to feel empowered. I finally understood I no longer had to play the victim. You could see the lights turning on in many people's faces. This epiphany was what we had all been waiting for.

The training finally came to a close. Patrick again thanked us for our extraordinary ability to participate and make a difference. We all stood up, and this time cheered loudly. Many people whistled. He got a little misty-eyed. He took a bow and blew kisses, said thank you one final time, and waived good-bye.

I strolled up to Patrick and let him know I would be at the Embassy Suites to meet him in an hour.

"Great, I'll meet you in the lobby." He leaned over and hugged me good-bye. "See you soon."

I was filled with this burst of sexual energy. Any fatigue or tiredness was completely gone now. I said my good-byes to everyone and hurried home to shower, shampoo, and shine. Plus, I needed to get my massage table and bag. I began to go from an excited state to complete and utter hysteria. The reality of it all was finally sinking in. I was going to finally be alone with him.

Chapter Eight

At home, I rushed around, getting myself together. I changed clothes and made sure to shave my legs. I lathered myself down with lotions, put some perfume on, brushed my teeth, and I was ready to go. I only had twenty minutes before I had to be there. I sped as fast as I could to get there on time. There are no words to fully express how I was feeling—ecstatic, euphoric weren't deep enough. Every thought of Patrick would bring up such a depth of love and excitement. I felt like every little particle in my body was being awakened. My senses heightened. I had no idea what kind of night this was going to be. I knew what I wanted. I had been waiting so long for someone like him to come into my life.

I pulled up to the valet in front of the hotel. I took my massage table and bag out of the car and then the driver drove off to park my car. My heart pounded. I really wanted Patrick to like my work. I was starting to feel nervous about what he would think. I walked into the lobby and there he stood. Walking straight up to me, he offered to take my table. We were always taught to never let clients carry the table. He insisted to take it up to his room, so I let him take over. He leaned over and gave me the biggest hug. It was warm and inviting and just what I needed to calm down and get back into my body. This time he wasn't teaching or doing private sessions. I was getting to see Patrick on a personal level.

We took the elevator up to his room. I shared with him how much I enjoyed the training and how what he did was incredible.

He smiled. "You know, you're the one who was really amazing." He had a way of making me feel so special and good about myself.

When we arrived in his room, I noticed that it was exactly like the one I had visualized. I began to wonder, *How much of this can really be true? Can I really create what I want with this man?* I set the massage table up and asked him all the questions about any boundaries that he may have in regards to getting his massage.

"I hardly ever let anyone work on me," he said. "It has been years since I've felt comfortable enough to trust someone to work on me."

"Thank you, I feel privileged."

"You have to be really great in order for me to let you do this. I have a feeling that you are that great."

"Thanks." I turned away to hide my embarrassment. I really hoped that I didn't disappoint him. I told him to get undressed, slip under the sheet, and start on the table face down.

"I'm going to wash my hands. I'll be right back." I went into the bathroom to take several deep breaths. Trying to center myself, I began to say a little prayer, "Dear God, please let me do my best work ever. Let him really enjoy what I do. Allow your spirit and healing to come through my hands so he too may feel as much nurturing, love, and healing as I felt when we did our session together. Thank you, Amen."

As I walked back into the room, I turned on the radio on his night stand to a station of smooth and relaxing jazz music. Then I approached the table and put my hand gently on his back.

"Take a deep breath," I said and proceeded to spread massage oil all over his soft, tanned skin. I was very intuitive, but always too shy and insecure to ever say anything to my clients if I picked up on something I was feeling. Within five minutes, I started to get this feeling about him.

Right as I picked up on it, he popped his head up out of the face cradle and asked, "What did you just get?"

I was taken aback. "I don't want to tell you."

"Why not?"

"What if I'm wrong?"

"What if you're not?" he replied.

"Okay . . . have you ever had a drug problem?"

"Yes, when I was a teenager. I was such a big pothead."

"Really! I was right?"

"You're really good. Keep going."

"Well, I feel like you had a lot of issues with your father. Is that true?"

"Yes, keep going."

I was freaking myself out. This was the first time that I had ever told anyone what I was picking up on them. I would feel so many things but I just didn't have the confidence to ever voice what I felt. I also was terrified if I was wrong. I kept massaging him and telling him for twenty minutes what I felt from his body. He confirmed everything. I asked him if he had major health problems that he hadn't shared with many people.

"Yes, you are absolutely right. I will tell you later."

Wow, I couldn't believe it. I was channeling all this information about him like I was this highly-tuned instrument. It was the most extraordinary thing that I had ever experienced in any of my healing sessions with someone.

"You are amazing!" he said. "This is the best body work I've ever had in my whole life"

"Really?" I was the best he ever had?

Patrick smiled. "You're unbelievable. I knew that you could do what I do. I want you to take all of my trainings."

I was speechless. I couldn't even take it all in. All I know is that I really enjoyed touching him to read his body and feel his energy. It was like I had stepped into another dimension—one I had never known before. Patrick felt very familiar. Our deep connection was something unexplainable and completely undeniable. I was totally in the healing zone for sure. I was so happy that he too was enjoying his session just as much as I was.

I was now ready to turn him over, face up. As he started to roll over, I saw these tiny silver sparkles coming out of his nose.

I gasped. "What the hell was that?" My jaw dropped and I took my hands off of him. "What was that?" I repeated.

"Sorry, so sorry," he said in this very fast voice.

I kept my distance from him.

"It's okay, Donza. It's okay."

"No way! What was that? I have to know what that just was."

He apologized again. "Just keep going. It's okay, really."

It was obvious that he wasn't going to tell me what those silver sparkles were.

"Is there anything else I need to know about you right now?" I asked.

"No, no, you can continue. You're doing such a great job."

I was a little nervous to touch him again, I must say. I really needed to know what that was coming out of his nose. He reached for my hand and gently squeezed it. He looked me straight in the eyes and smiled this buttery-warm smile that made my heart melt. He stared longer than usual. You know that look when you know someone is attracted to you? If there had been any doubts in mind how he felt up to now, that one look definitely spoke volumes.

I continued with the session, keeping quiet now, allowing

him to just relax and absorb everything I was doing. Also, I had to make sure I remained professional. Any flirtatious talking would make it much harder to concentrate and get through it. I finished the session with these light, gentle, nurturing caresses with the tips of my fingers called "nerve strokes." He loved them. They also would clear his auric field and help relax him even more.

"I have never had anything like this before," he said. "You are truly excellent at what you do. I am so impressed."

His praising words kept firing off in my head like a thousand bottle rockets shooting high up in the sky.

"Now, just relax," I said. "I'm going to wash my hands. You can slowly get up when you're ready. There's no rush."

I went into the bathroom. I was vibrating all over. I was shaking on the inside because so far everything I had visualized had happened, just the way I envisioned it. Did this mean he was now going to make a move and try to kiss me? Well, he wouldn't have to try at all. I knew he would just do it. This was going to be the night that all of my dreams came true. When I came out of the bathroom he was wearing this terry cloth, white robe and standing in front of the bed. I started taking the table down and asked him how he was feeling.

"Incredible. I really needed that more than I realized."

"I'm so happy you're feeling better." I put the table by the door in its carrying case. As I walked over to him he reached his arms out to give me a hug. The energy that was expelling from both of our bodies was electric. He held me close. I gently pushed him back on the bed and was now lying on top of him. I kissed him on the lips as quickly as humanly possible and then buried my face in his neck. I shocked myself. *I* was the one making the first move! The fact that I actually had the nerve to do that was extraordinary. I then stood up fast and started to blush. He knew what a big deal that was for me too.

"Would you like to go get some dinner with me now?" he asked.

"Yes. Let me take my table down to my car while you get dressed."

"No way, I'll carry it down for you."

I waited there for him to get ready. As he went into the bathroom I decided to go into the living room. I sat on the soft, cozy sofa and waited. My mind and heart were both racing fast. I couldn't stop thinking about those silver sparkles flying out of his nostrils. I also couldn't believe how I was able to know all of those things about him. I really was able to do some of what Patrick did in his session. I sat there in utter amazement at myself. I wondered if I would be able to read someone else's body as well as I did his. This was the first time I ever had the confidence or worked on someone who made me feel comfortable enough to explore my intuition. I hoped that I could do this with my other clients. I really wanted to learn everything that Patrick was teaching, especially if he thought I could do it too.

He opened the bathroom door and stepped out. He was now dressed in all black—really nice slacks and a button-down shirt with a pair of stylish Armani shoes. I could smell his sweet scent all the way from the other room. He smelled liked an angel.

I walked up to him. "You smell incredible. What cologne are you wearing?"

"Halston Z-14."

I leaned in and took another sniff. "Wow, that is the best ever."

"Thanks, glad you like it." He smiled. "Are you ready to go?"

"Sure."

He then picked up my table and I carried my massage bag. We headed down to the valet to get my car. I felt relieved that we were taking the table down. With my work gear put away I could enjoy the evening more fully. Whatever was going to happen at least my table was out of the room. I had never allowed a client to take my table out nor had I ever gone to dinner with one either. I didn't feel like he was just my client, since I had spent so much time with him over the weekend and during our private session. We were trading sessions and I wasn't getting paid. I rationalized that it was okay to have dinner with him. Also, I don't think I could have ever turned him down.

We decided to go to the restaurant at the hotel. By this time I was feeling nervous. I didn't want to say anything wrong. I wanted to keep impressing him. I didn't know how or what else I could do. We sat down at a very nice table with a white table cloth and a candle burning in the center. He came over and pulled my chair out. So sweet and thoughtful. As we sat down I asked how he was feeling.

"The best that I've felt in a long time. You're incredible. Not many people can do what you do."

"Thank you so much."

"Are you starting to get who you are yet?"

I smiled and shrugged my shoulders. I was starting to feel a little shy and self-conscious. I hoped that he wouldn't be complimenting me as much as the last time. Most young women would have loved it. For me it was just too much to take in.

"Would you like a drink?" he offered

"No thank you. I don't drink. I really don't care for the taste."

He ordered a drink for himself and asked again if I wanted a drink.

"No. I don't, thank you." I was a fitness trainer and didn't feel well if I did. "Do you drink often?" I asked.

"No, not much at all. I just smoke."

This made me cringe. I would have much preferred a drinker than a smoker for sure. Well, not an alcoholic or anything. I then began asking him personal questions like: where are you from originally? How long have you been In L.A.? Anything I could think of. I wanted to know everything. He was now answering back, talking much more about himself than ever before. I loved listening to everything he had to say.

"I was born and raised in New Mexico, though I've been working in California for years. I've traveled all over the world and done many trainings overseas." He lit up when he talked about his travels. I then asked him to tell me about his health issues.

"When I was a little boy my parents wanted a girl. My mother even said how the doctor yelled out at my birth, 'Wrong, it's a boy!'" He had shared this story at the training. "For years I had to have my penis hole opened and reopened several times as a small child. It was very painful and I remember being very frightened. What I didn't share is that when I was nineteen I was diagnosed with prostate cancer. They told us that I only had six months to live. My parents were in shock and I went completely numb. I was already smoking a lot of pot and this news sent me on a downward spiral. I thought that if I'm going to die, at least I won't feel any of the pain. I was young and naïve.

"Then I heard about a woman coming to town who did a process called rebirthing. It was a breathing technique that was supposed to clear any childhood issues and birth trauma. I was open to trying anything that might help. She also was taking a few chosen students to India for some of her trainings and to teach people how to do rebirthing. She told my parents that she thought this trip could save my life. They agreed to pay for my trip and all of the trainings I would be taking. I was skeptical for sure. I was also too high to really get the impact that this was all going to have on my life. Then the woman told me that I had to stop smoking pot if I wanted to go. Would I be willing to give it up? At first, I said no way. There was this voice deep within me that said I must go."

I was hanging on to every word. I leaned in with my arms resting on the table, totally enthralled with his life story.

"In order to understand this fully, Donza, I must tell you more about my childhood. Let's wait until after dinner and I'll tell you everything."

"Oh, no you can't stop there. I have to know what happens."

He smiled and I could plainly see how he really enjoyed leaving me hanging.

"You're really going to make me wait?" I asked.

"Yes, I am." He winked.

"Okay, I see how you are." Our chemistry was really strong now. I couldn't help wondering if anything was going to happen between us tonight. I hoped that he would make a move. He already knew I was into him. What else did he need? What was he waiting for? The anticipation was almost more than I could handle.

By this time we had ordered our food and he was halfway finished with his drink. He seemed more relaxed now. He turned the conversation towards me and started asking questions about my life. This time about my relationships.

"Are you involved with anyone?" he asked.

"No, I'm not. How about you?"

"No, I haven't made the time with all of my traveling. It's hard to find someone who can understand my schedule."

"That must be hard on you."

He shrugged. "No, not really because I love my work. I'll find time for a relationship later. What about you? Why aren't you with someone?"

"Well, I have only had one relationship ever. I was a late bloomer. Also, I was always too shy to tell anyone what I was feeling. Although, I have to admit, after this weekend I am starting to feel much more confident and secure about myself."

"Really? You have only been with one man?"

I couldn't believe he just flat out asked me that. Now, I was really embarrassed. "Yes. Just one."

"How long were you with him?"

"I knew him for a long while before anything ever happened. He went to school with me. We weren't together long—off and on for several months."

Now he was leaning in, his eyes never leaving mine. The chemistry between us seemed to intensify. I so badly wanted him to reach across that table and kiss me.

If he doesn't make a move by the end of dinner, will I have to do it? Do I even have the nerve to attempt it again?

I was putting so much pressure on myself. I took a deep breath. Okay, girl, just put those thoughts out of your mind for now.

"So, Patrick, I have a question for you. What exactly were those sparkles coming out of your nose? I've never seen anything like that before."

"I apologize for that."

"Well, what was it?"

"It's not time for you to know about that yet."

"What! Are you serious? You're not going to tell me?"

"No, I'm not. Not right now."

"Patrick, when are you going to tell me?"

"Some day," he replied with a devilish grin.

It was driving me crazy! He definitely knew how to get me hyped up. And he was enjoying it too.

By this time our food arrived and I was feeling very frustrated. Not only would he not tell me his deepest secrets, he still hadn't made a move yet. I began to wonder if all the feelings I was having were just mine.

Was I totally wrong about everything? Did he not have feelings for me? If so, was he ever going to show it?

Within seconds, he reached over and touched my hand.

"Would you like to have some dessert?" he asked.

"No thank you. I'm not a big sugar eater."

"Then would you like to continue our conversation in my room?"

I nodded, trying to contain my excitement. Was my fantasy really going to happen tonight?

He paid the bill and I thanked him for a lovely dinner. As we started walking toward the elevators, I could feel the nervousness spreading throughout my body. I was trembling inside. I was very inexperienced and self-conscious. Was I even going to be able to handle this? I had been fantasizing about being intimate with Patrick for days now. I somehow had to relax and let go.

He flirted on the way up to his room, actually teasing me about how embarrassed I was becoming. He thought it was sexy.

"Stop teasing," I said.

He just smiled as we arrived at his room. As he opened the door and motioned for me to go in first, I paused at the threshold.

Leaning in, he whispered, "Dorothy, surrender, give me your shoes." Then he started kissing me. It felt right out of a movie. The passion and intensity were overwhelming. I had never felt anything like this before. The build up to this moment couldn't even compare to what I was actually feeling. This was the best kiss I had ever had in my life! I felt like I was dreaming. He was so into it that I couldn't even believe it myself. He held my face with his tender hands and kept kissing me for a long time. It awakened a passion inside me that I never knew existed. My body was on fire. The energy between us felt like a volcano had just erupted. He had the softest lips ever.

His lovely cologne swept over me like an ocean wave. I was truly captivated by his essence. His presence was intoxicating. His passion stimulating. I was being turned on to a whole new level of sexual awareness. I felt like Alice in Wonderland tumbling down the rabbit hole, wondering how far I was going to fall. Then Patrick picked me up off my feet and carried me to the bed. As he lay me gently down, my whole body trembled. I was losing myself in this magical moment. He was taking me into a whole new realm, one that I wasn't familiar with at all. Although I was completely over-joyed and thrilled that my fantasies were coming true, I prayed that I would be able to be fully self-expressed in the deepest and most intimate way.

He started slowly kissing down my neck. I felt tremors throughout my body. Strong sexual feelings illuminated my total being. I was set free from this world of control and limitations. Feeling comfortable and safe, I could now allow myself to enjoy him. At this point, all of the lights were still on in the bedroom.

I whispered in his ear, "Can we turn the lights off please?"

"No way! I want to see every inch of that beautiful body of yours."

What, is he joking? I'd never had the lights on before. I was always way too self-conscious. Now I thought I was going to die inside. *I have to get over myself. I am a grown woman who is mad for this man.* I could tell by his passionate kisses that he was just as crazy about me too.

As he kept slowly kissing and undressing me I began to sur-render. I closed my eyes and took some deep breaths. I was acutely present to every move he was making and to all of the explosions firing off inside me. He complimented every small detail of my body, helping me feel more relaxed and at ease. I let go a little more with each exploring kiss. Our bodies merged together. I could also feel his hunger and deep desire burning within. He was in total control and, for the first time, I loved it.

Until this moment I hadn't known what it was like to make love or to be made love to. This was absolutely the most incredible feeling ever. Finally, I had met a man who was attuned and sensitive to my needs. I became aware of my body drowning delightfully in his sea of sexual seduction. Time didn't exist. The only thing that mattered was the rapture between us. Moans of pleasure began to slowly release from my mouth. I slipped away into another dimension, one where I could be totally free and self-expressed. I was no longer a prisoner in my body or my mind. Something had taken over. It was love. This energy completely encompassed me. I had no idea where I started or where Patrick began. Our spirits became one. Total bliss. I felt this unconditional love for him, for myself, for the Universe, and for God. It was so powerful and truly one of the most difficult things to describe. Words just seem too limiting.

This night with Patrick embedded such a deep, profound impact on my soul. This was my first true spiritual experience. It wasn't just sex. It was the beginning of a romantic love that changed my life and opened my heart to a whole new level of depth and passion.

* * *

Hours had gone by and Patrick finally turned out the lights. By that time I didn't even notice them anymore. It was such an amazing feeling to be enthralled with one another. As I lay wrapped in his arms, not wanting to part in any way, my thoughts began to wonder about our future together. Would we be able to do a long-distance relationship? Did he even want to be with me after tonight? Could he be the one I would spend the rest of my life with? Only time would tell.

He was now lying on his back. I pressed my head onto his chest and snuggled up close. I could hear his heart beating in my ear. It was very comforting. I felt completely relaxed being there with him. I began to ponder my own mystical experiences before I met this man who had brought me further into the knowledge of love, sex, mysticism, and the reality beyond the senses. I wondered if my life had begun to take on a new meaning. All of my experiences before this moment seemed insignificant now. Perhaps it was because Patrick was so conscious and aware, or maybe it was because I felt this awakening inside with each touch we exchanged. In any case, I had finally stepped into the void with another living, breathing person. Inside this alternate realm I was discovering myself for the very first time. I was being reborn and it felt incredible. I had been searching for this kind of spirit to help unleash my many gifts, talents, and healing abilities. He was able to go to those places within and help open me up to my fullest potential. I was no longer the same woman who I had once believed I was. I could no longer hide behind my ego, fears, limitations, and many shortcomings. It was time to experience my true self and the powerful gifts I received that night. Many questions kept going through my mind as I was lying there in his arms.

He must have felt it because he asked, "What are you thinking about?"

"You," I said.

"Really? What about me?"

"I'm still curious about what happened to you in India and how you overcame your illness." I must have had more energy than him because he began to yawn, and I felt him slip away to a restful, peaceful place.

He leaned down and kissed my head. "Can we talk more about this in the morning?"

It took a long time for me to fall asleep. He was a snuggler. He wrapped his legs around my legs and spooned my body the entire night. I could not have imagined this night going as perfectly as it did. Even though I had wanted him badly, there was a part of me that couldn't believe my prayers were being answered and that I could potentially have the man of my dreams.

Chapter Nine

The next morning I woke up to fingers lightly caressing my shoulders and lips kissing my neck. He then moved in to kiss my lips, but I was too worried about morning breath.

"Hold that thought." I crawled out of bed and went into the bathroom. I found his toothpaste on the side of sink and gave my mouth a quick wash using my finger as a toothbrush. As I opened the door he was standing there with his arms open wide, offering the most loving and tender hug. He went into the bathroom and told me to get back in bed. I could hear the water in the sink running. He was brushing his teeth too. It was kind of sweet.

He slid back under the covers, pulled me close to him, and started kissing me so passionately again. Both of our mouths tasted fresh. Sweet . . . and minty. His lips seemed to fit perfectly with mine. Once again we had another hour of pure pleasure. Afterwards, he reached for a cigarette. It was like a scene right out of a movie.

"How are you feeling?" he asked.

"I'm feeling great." I thought now would be a good time for him to close all of the open loops he had going on. So I asked again, "What happened to you in India?"

"One of the things I never told you was that when I was a young boy I would dream about this child. He would come to me and tell me things when I was awake and in my dreams."

"What kind of things?" I asked.

"Well, when my little sister fell on the playground and broke her arm, I could hear this boy telling me how to hold her arm and fix it. When we took my sister to the hospital the doctors asked, 'Who helped her?' I answered, 'Me.' I then drew a picture of my sister's arm to show them what it looked like before I moved it back into place. The doctors were shocked. They were completely blown away. 'How could you know how to do this?' I didn't tell them anything about the image of this boy that was often present, guiding me through it.

"The doctors then wanted to do all these tests on me to find out what else I could do. That's when we discovered that my left brain wasn't functioning the same as my right. That my main usage was my right brain. The doctors would then take me into a patient's room and I would look at them and scan my hands over their body and say, 'You have a tennis ball in your tummy,' and it would wind up being an ulcer. Or I would touch their head and feel a bump in their head and it would be some kind of a tumor. This went on for years. So I began at an early age listening to my intuition and this boy in my dreams. When I was eleven, my family and I moved to another city. My mother said, 'Now you can't do this weird stuff here.' I began to feel like I was some kind of freak. At thirteen I started playing music and smoking a lot of pot. I wanted to disappear and ignore everything I was feeling.

"So when I arrived in India with prostrate cancer and with the thought of having only six months to live, this was a wake up call, to say the least. My mentor took me to an ashram to meet this guru. As I walked in, there were several pictures on the wall of many different Indian gurus. Then I saw this picture of the young boy in my dreams hanging on the wall in front of me. I started to panic. Who was this child that had been visiting me for years? The guru walked in at this moment, looked straight into my eyes, and said, 'I've been waiting for you.' I was still feeling overwhelmed from seeing this photograph of the boy on the wall."

By this time I was so captivated by Patrick's story that I was now sitting up in the bed with my legs across his. He continued describing the photograph of the boy from his dreams. "'Who is that?' I asked my guru.

'That is Babaji as a child.'

'Who was Babaji?'

'He is our guru. You will learn many things about him while you are here.' The guru then smiled and asked me, 'Do you want to live?'

'Of course I do.'

He said, 'Then you must listen and do everything I tell you. Can you do that?'

'Sure,' I answered, not having a clue of what was going to happen next.

The guru then told me that I would have to go out in the desert and fast and feel all of the pain that was in my body.

'I don't feel any pain,' I told him.

He then gave me this hose to take with me. He told me to use it when I became angry.

'I'm not angry.'

'Go now,' he said.

The only thing I had with me was water and this long black hose. I was then dropped off in the hot scorching desert. Sand was blowing in my face and hair. Sun blazing on my skin. I was not a happy camper. I didn't quite know what I was supposed to be doing here. I had never really meditated before in my life, nor had I ever fasted. As I sat in the sweltering heat, my mind wondered how this was going to help me. After the first twenty-four hours I was exhausted. By the second day I was becoming agitated and starting to feel extremely upset. Finally, by the third day my anger had turned to rage. I took that hose and started beating it for hours. I yelled and screamed and kept beating the sand with that hose until finally I fell to my knees and broke down into tears. It was the most cathartic feeling ever. Then it rang through my head how I was wrong for being a boy. All of these thoughts kept flooding through my mind until finally I put it together that I had been unconsciously punishing myself for being a boy. I cried for hours until I eventually fell asleep on the sand. When I awoke, the guru's people were there to bring me back to the ashram. I had never been so drained and exhausted, and at the same time I felt lighter and free from years of emotional baggage and pain.

"When I arrived at the ashram, the guru took one look at me and said, 'You're healed. Go soak yourself in a hot bath.' That's all he said. I was too fatigued to argue. They escorted me to a bath that had been drawn up by his many devotees. As I sank down into this bath filled with herbs, my head was pounding. I soaked for about fifteen minutes. Then, all of sudden I was in severe pain. My stomach started cramping. I felt like I was going to faint. Then this brown liquid secreted out of my penis. I think I went into shock at this point. All of the pain I was feeling went completely away. I knew the cancer was leaving my body."

Patrick paused and I shook my head. "Wow, that's the most incredible story I've ever heard. You need to write a book about this." His story was hard to believe, but I had sat and watched him tell it. I knew it was all true every word of it. "You were healed of cancer then?" I asked.

"After the bath I went to talk to the master guru. He reassured me again that I was healed. I was the biggest skeptic too at this time in my life. I was only nineteen. The next day I went to a doctor in

India and they ran their tests. Indeed I was healed. There was no sign of any prostate cancer. This was when I knew what I was supposed to do the rest of my life. To help people heal. Learn everything I could about the subconscious mind and to use my healing abilities to change the world. I stayed in India for two years, learning and becoming a professional rebirther. I started working on people privately with my sessions. It was the most profound work I had ever experienced."

"You are incredible," I said. "Thank you so much for sharing your story. I could listen to you all day long." I leaned over and kissed him once again. I felt closer to him after he shared his childhood story with me. I never wanted to leave that room. I wanted to stay in this beautiful, intimate world that we had created together—a sacred space where we could both be completely open and vulnerable. Now there was only one more question that had been dwelling in my mind since the night before.

"Now please, please tell me . . . What in the world was flying out of your nose?"

He smiled. "Some things we aren't supposed to know until we're ready."

Chapter Ten

It was early morning and Patrick was leaving for L.A. today. I did my best not to think about him going. The sheer thought made me feel sad and sick to my stomach. I wasn't much for good-byes. His plane was taking off at noon and he asked if I wanted to drive him to the airport.

"Of course, I do."

"Good," he smiled. "Let's order room service and have some breakfast. How does that sound?"

That sounded great to me. I thought now would be the time to check in with him and find out where we were. I was a little nervous to bring up the conversation. Actually, very nervous, and scared, but I knew I had to know where we stood.

"So when are you coming back to Dallas?"

"I'm not sure," he said. "I'm training in L.A. I want you to be there if you can."

"When?"

"In eight weeks. I will be traveling for the next four weeks to different cities doing trainings and private sessions."

My heart sank. I looked down and I turned away from him.

He caught my reaction. "Can I call you from each city?"

My spirit lifted again. "Yes, I would like that." I could feel my insecurities coming up.

He wrapped his arms around me. "You are very special and I want you to know how beautiful and powerful you are."

"Thank you," I whispered.

He then kissed my cheek. "Now let's order some breakfast."

* * *

As we sat down to eat together, I was feeling happy and content with each conversation and every moment we shared. My feelings for him were growing stronger and deeper than I could have ever imagined. Love was blossoming inside of me.

The time had come for me to take him to the airport. This was probably the most difficult thing I've ever had to do. As the bags were being loaded up in the trunk of my car, I was feeling like I was going to break down and cry. I knew I had to hold it together. I didn't want to show too much of my feelings at this point. Also, I knew he could feel how sad I was about his leaving. As we got into my car, he leaned over and held my hand and gave me a tender kiss. I smiled then drove away from the hotel. Patrick held my hand the whole way while I was driving. I was very quiet. I didn't want to talk because I was afraid I would lose it right in front of him. The elixir of emotions stirring inside me was unpredictable. I had never said good-bye to someone I felt this strongly about.

He told me what an amazing time he had and that he couldn't wait to be with me again. Just knowing this was difficult for him, too, cheered me up a little.

He put his hand on my thigh. "How are you feeling?"

My face tightened to hold back any emotions. I nodded and said, "I'm okay," even though I knew he could see right through me.

He squeezed my hand. "You're better than okay. You're perfect."

I pulled up in front of the drop-off lane at DFW Airport. I asked, "Do you have a picture of yourself you could give to me?" I remembered seeing one that they had displayed at the training.

"Yes," he said. We both got out of the car. He pulled his luggage out of my trunk and reached into his bag. He handed me an 8 x 10 black and white headshot. He looked gorgeous. He took out a pen and wrote something on the photo for me. Then he opened the passenger car door and placed the photo on the seat.

"You can read it when I leave."

I walked around the car and we stood there staring into each other's eyes. I could feel the tears starting to well up as he wrapped his loving arms around me. We held each other tight. I didn't want to ever let him go. He gave me one more passionate, long, incredible kiss. One of those kisses that make your heart feel as though it's going to stop beating at any moment. As I stood there a thousand memories flashed through my head, like a camera snapping each shot frame by frame of our time together. I couldn't hold back the tears any longer. I had to get out of there or it was going to be one of those intense, ugly cries that you pray no one ever sees. I pulled back from him, fighting back the tears.

He placed his hands on my cheeks and gently wiped away my tears. Then he kissed me again. "I will see you soon and talk with you later."

I smiled. "Thank you for everything."

"No, thank you! You are so incredible."

We embraced one more time before he picked up his luggage and turned to walk in through the airport doors. I stood there waiting for him to look back. He did and then blew me one more kiss.

I rushed to my car to see what he had written on his picture.

To Donza, on a scale of one to ten. You're a perfect twelve! Love, Patrick.

I placed the photo against my chest, as if I was hugging him one final time. That's when I lost it. Tears poured down my face.

I drove away from the airport. I placed his picture across my lap. Somehow it seemed to make me feel better having it there. I had never been deeply intimate with someone and then had them leave right after. It left me feeling unsettled.

Would he call in a few days like he said he would? Would I be able to afford to go see him in L.A? Would we be able to have a relationship together?

I felt exhausted. I allowed myself to cry the whole way home. Along with my sadness, I was also feeling blessed and grateful for our time together. I was very young and unsure how to deal with the depth of emotion that Patrick had awakened inside me. I also felt that he was out of my league on so many levels and that maybe I didn't deserve to have a man like this in my life. To be honest, I still had a lot of work to do on myself, especially when it came to self worth, self esteem, and relationships. Spending this kind of time and intimacy with Patrick really helped my confidence. His private work and seminar were so insightful and life changing that I could literally feel something inside had shifted and let go deep within my spirit. I felt reborn.

PART TWO
Long Distance

Chapter Eleven

Three days passed and I had not heard from Patrick yet. I was worried and began to have thoughts of inadequacy and fear at the same time. I found myself waiting around as much as I could for the phone to ring. Each time it did ring I would race to answer it. The disappointment of it not being him was almost unbearable. I wondered if he was ever going to call or be in contact with me again. So many crazy thoughts were going off in my mind. Did he have other women in different cities? Did what we share mean anything to him at all?

I was becoming more and more agitated with each passing hour. I finally had to put all of those thoughts behind me for now. He was in California so there was a two-hour time change, although I had told him that he could call at any time. He had reassured that he would call. He did not give me a specific day or time. I kept wishing I would have been clearer with him about it. As I started to get ready for bed, I was feeling sad. I just knew that he wasn't going to call and that I had just been played by this incredible, sexy healer who had come to town. I didn't even get his phone number so there wasn't any way to contact him. Not like I would have ever called him or anything. I was raised that a woman never calls the man. She waits till the man calls her.

It was looking like I wasn't going to be in contact with him again if he didn't call. I then crawled into bed and turned out the lights. It was almost eleven p.m. All of the sudden the phone rang. I really didn't think anything of it. All my friends knew that I was a night owl. I was expecting it to be my friend Tori calling. We often had late night, phone-conversation rituals to fill each other in on our busy days. I answered the phone and said, "Hey girl, what are you doing?"

"Donza, is that you?"

Oh my God, it was him! He had this very soft-spoken voice. I could barely hear him.

"Patrick? Is that really you?" My voice went up three octaves.

"It's me."

I couldn't stop smiling. I was so happy to hear his voice.

"How are you, Donza?"

"I'm great now! How are you?"

"You've been worried, haven't you?"

I wanted to say, "No, what do you mean?" But he would have known I was lying. I answered, "Yes, I was a little concerned that I hadn't heard anything for three days."

"I'm so sorry I didn't call you earlier. I've been working non-stop and haven't had a moment of rest. I've thought about you often."

"Oh really?" I asked. "What have you been thinking about?"

"When I am going to see you again? Are you going to be able to come to Los Angeles for my training?"

"I'm not sure yet." I didn't want to tell him how broke I was and that I really couldn't afford to go.

"When will you know?"

"Soon, I hope."

He told me again what a great time he had and that he couldn't wait to see me again. By this time I was sitting up in bed with the lights turned on. I could almost smell him in the room. What I remember most about our conversation is that I never wanted it to end. My ear was pressed hard against the receiver as I sat there listening to every word he was saying. He had such a gentle and peaceful voice. It was very soothing, like cherry cough syrup to a swollen throat. We talked for over an hour. He told me this was a really big deal for him, because he didn't like talking on the phone.

"Why?" I asked.

"I'll tell you later, when we're together."

I was a talker and loved chatting on the phone for hours when I had the time. He never had the time to do so.

"I will make the time for you," he said. I'm sure he could feel my smiling energy through the phone. With each moment we were on the phone together, I felt my heart opening up more than before. These were the most intense feelings I had ever felt for anyone. I wanted to tell him badly how much I was feeling for him. I just couldn't at this time. The fact was that I had never opened up my heart like this before. He had to have known since he was highly intuitive.

He began to go over our time together and telling his favorite moments that we shared. This was the best part of our conversation. It was nice to hear a man talking about his feelings so freely and with no hesitation at all. This was very unfamiliar to me.

"I feel very comfortable with you," he said. "Believe it or not, Donza, I used to be very shy and I wouldn't talk to women until after I was out of high school."

"Are you serious?"

"Yes, completely. I used to wear these Coke-bottle glasses as a child and I was stick-thin and looked like I was twelve years old when I was eighteen."

"Really?" I couldn't believe it. I told him, "I used to be cross-eyed and wore glasses until I was eleven years old. I had the body of a ten year old when I was sixteen."

"Interesting. How did they fix your eyes?"

"I had surgery on both of them when I was eleven. It was an amazing success story. The doctors used my eyes as an example for others that had my same problem." I had no idea that we would have so much in common.

Patrick said, "I was very attracted to you when I saw you walk into the room. You weren't even looking up at the front of the class."

"I know," I said. "When I did, I was stunned. I was overwhelmed when I looked at you."

"You were?" he asked.

"Yes, I must confess I thought you were the most beautiful man I had ever seen." *Wait, did I really just tell him what I thought? Yes, I did.* I was feeling really embarrassed.

"How are you feeling now?" he asked.

"Exposed and vulnerable."

"I really like it when you're open and honest with me."

"Thank you," I said. "I've never met anyone like you before. This is all very new for me." I was unaccustomed to talking about my feelings and actually sharing them with someone, especially a man. I was taught to never trust or open up your feelings too fast. "That's how we women get our hearts broken," my mother used to tell me. I know she was just trying to be protective and helpful.

With Patrick it was easy to be open, honest, and completely myself. I wanted to know all I could about him and, believe it or not, I wanted to share everything about my life with him too. He had a way of making me feel so special. Maybe it was because whenever I was with him he was totally present, seemingly not thinking of anything else. I knew he was only interested in getting to know me and learn about my life. I also knew that I had much to learn from him. He was the most spiritual, intelligent, and absolutely the most insightful person I had ever met. I still found it hard to believe that he was attracted to me. I didn't feel like I would be able to teach him anything, or that I would be enough. I finally told him that when we were talking.

"That is your birth script coming up again," he said. "After you clear that out and realize how special and powerful you are, you are going to be amazed at how you will feel."

"It's hard to even imagine. You must be getting tired of telling me these things because I can't seem to believe them."

"No, not at all. I will keep telling you until you get it."

"I'm just afraid that you are too good to be true and that you are going to get tired of all of my insecurities."

"Not a chance." That made me smile. I was in complete bliss after talking for an hour. He said that he would call soon and that he couldn't wait to see me again.

"I can't wait to see you too, Patrick."

He gave me a big kiss over the phone and I puckered up my lips and sent a gigantic one back to him. As I hung up, I felt as if I were now becoming a real woman. I was falling in love for the first time and enjoying every nuance of this experience. I rolled over and looked at his picture on the night stand. My heart was full as I turned out the lights.

Chapter Twelve

Several more days passed without hearing from him. I was trying to figure a way to make enough money to go to his training in L.A. I had just gotten my massage business going and was also teaching gymnastics part-time, which didn't pay much at all. I started doing fitness training a few hours a week to make ends meet. I even waited tables two nights a week. I was working four jobs, seven days a week and loved it. You would think that I would be making tons of money, but I was barely scraping by. I had gotten into debt and was working hard to get out of it. I had secretly hoped that Patrick would call and offer me a plane ticket out there. But I never let him know how much I was struggling. I just couldn't.

Now a week had gone by and still not a word from him. I decided to ask several of my new massage clients to buy a package of massages from me to help me out. Three of my clients said "yes." I was now manifesting all the money that I needed to go on this trip. I took a leap of faith and bought my plane ticket. I planned to stay one extra day so I'd be able to hopefully spend some quality time with Patrick, even though I didn't know his schedule. I was trusting that it was all going to work out. I was starting to feel excited about going to California. I couldn't wait to see him in his own town.

Two weeks passed and still I hadn't heard from him. I was starting to get a little concerned. *Did he forget about me?* I thought he would have called sooner after our last conversation. I knew he was a very busy man and he also had a private practice that was booming. He told me that he had a lot to get done and that he would be talking to me soon. What was soon to him obviously had a whole different meaning to me. I so badly wanted to call him. But I didn't get his number when we last talked. Again, I found myself waiting by the phone. I was so eager to tell him that I was going to be coming to his training and that I would be seeing him soon. I also couldn't wait to kiss him again and just be close to him. Those thoughts helped ease my worry and frustration a little.

By the beginning of week three, I still hadn't heard from him at all. I felt deflated. I had bought the ticket already. I had arranged a place to stay with a friend who was living there. I had no idea where the seminar was going to be held, and time was running out. Why hadn't he called?

I didn't like this one bit. I made the decision that if he did call I would totally give him a piece of my mind. He couldn't just blow me off like this. That's what I was feeling at the time. That he didn't really care. He was just wanting a fun time and that was it. Though it felt so real when we were together. Even our last phone conversation was wonderful and I felt connected to him. What had changed?

Finally, that evening the phone rang. I didn't even run to get it at this point. I answered and there he was.

"Hey, sexy." That's what he said, as if no time had passed at all.

"Hello, stranger. Where have you been?"

He immediately started to apologize for not calling sooner. "I had to go out of town."

"They don't have phones where you were?" I asked in a very short tone.

"Yes, they do. My father is dying." Now I felt like such a jerk. How could I have known?

"I'm so sorry. How are you doing?"

"I am doing okay. I have had a lot going on."

"Are you still having your training?" I asked.

"Yes, I am. Are you going to make it?"

"Yes, I will be there."

"I am so happy to hear that! That news has made my day." Just knowing that he was happy that I was going and that we were going to be seeing each other very soon made me smile.

"I can't wait to see you," he said.

"Me too!"

He then gave all the details to his training and asked where I would be staying. I was hoping that he would want me to stay with him. Right as that thought came into my head, he said, "I am staying at the hotel where the training is. I would love for you to stay with me, though I am going to be too busy working. I also have to be careful that people don't think I'm seeing one of my students."

"What people?"

"I don't usually date my clients."

I was relieved to hear that. "Will I get to see you after the training?"

"Yes, of course. I'm really excited that you're coming to L.A. We're going to have a lot of fun."

Finally, I asked if I could get his number.

"Sure."

We talked for a while longer and I knew he truly meant what he had said. He was excited to see me, maybe just as much as I was to see him. We then said our good-byes once again. This time was different, though. I felt that we were in a better place. Closer than we were before and a new level of trust was happening between us. I knew he was going to be way too busy to call me again before I left. I told him that I would see him soon. "I miss you" were his final words to me that night. Of course, I said the same thing back and smiled as I hung up the phone.

Chapter Thirteen

The day had come to leave for L.A. I had worked hard to finally get it all together to go. I was so proud of myself. I was also filled with enthusiasm and this overwhelming feeling of anticipation. I couldn't wait to see him again, also to be learning his new healing modalities and techniques. This was a totally different seminar than the one he gave in Dallas. I wanted to know everything that he taught. Now, it looked like I was going to be getting exactly what I wanted. I felt like I had found the man of my dreams and it was only a matter of time that he would soon realize I was The One. I was hoping, anyway. Everything that I had visualized had come true so far. I was giving all of this New Age thinking a try now. Why not? It seemed to be working.

As I finished packing my bags and getting ready to go to the airport, this intense fear started to creep into my bones. I hated flying. I had a close call when I was seventeen that forever changed my experience of flying. I was truly phobic about it. I would literally tremble and my body would shake whenever the plane would run into turbulence. I would grab hold of a complete stranger and hang on for dear life. Each time I flew I warned my neighbors sitting next to me that I was a big baby when it came to flying. I thought for sure I was going to be sick just from the sheer thought of getting on another plane. I wished that I would have told Patrick about my fear of flying. He could have said just the perfect words to help calm my nerves. But he had already seen many of my flaws. I didn't want to amplify any more of my fears or anything that might make me look bad. I was on my own now.

I arrived two hours early at the airport. I wanted to make sure that I didn't have any problems with check-in or baggage. I always seemed to over pack. This trip was no exception. It was the late Eighties and our bad hair days were still very much in. That meant a whole lot of hair products. As I went through security I was getting nervous again. I was all alone and could feel myself starting to freak out a little bit. I rushed as fast as I could through security, trying to get to my gate as quickly as possible. I thought if I could just sit and relax that might calm me down.

I finally made it. I had over an hour to wait before takeoff. What could I do to ease my tension and fear? I brought a notebook with me and decided that I would journal my thoughts and feelings about flying, about Patrick, the seminar, and what I was about to face. I would often write about my deepest feelings and desires. I never read them to anyone. As I began journaling, I started to calm down. I never used writing before to relax, so this was a new tool that seemed to have a powerful effect on my emotional state. I wondered if I should keep a journal of my time in Los Angeles. I remembered keeping a diary as a young girl and that one of my siblings stole it. I never did get that diary back. Since then I didn't journal or write very often. I thought this trip would be a great time to start again. I was a grown woman and had no siblings around to worry about stealing my diary.

Time seemed to fly by while I was writing, because the next thing I heard was, "Boarding for Los Angeles." Wow, it had worked. I was now calmer than before. My plan was to just keep writing while on the plane, as long as there was no turbulence.

I found my seat swiftly. I sank down in the soft, cozy, red chair and waited for takeoff. I must confess, I began getting scared again. I had heard that the takeoffs and landings were the most dangerous and if you wait two minutes after the flight gets going, then you will be all right. I thought I had better pay attention to those important two minutes. You just never know, right? The pilot came on and spoke in this deep, low base tone. I knew in that moment that everything was going to be just fine. The flight went smoothly and we arrived on time.

I was so excited to be in L.A. My girlfriend was there waiting to pick me up at the gate. It was also a treat to be seeing her too. I had told her the whole story about Patrick. I wanted her to go to the training, but she had to work. Once again I was on my own. I was a little nervous about going to another seminar, especially since Patrick and I had crossed those professional boundaries. I wasn't sure if I could contain my excitement and be just another person in the class. I was going to have to really make an effort. I wondered how he was going to be acting towards me since he had to remain professional too. I was happy that I didn't have long to wait.

Chapter Fourteen

Finally, the morning of the seminar came and I was feeling all this anxiety. I was now in his city and I felt like I had no control over anything. Everything was new and unfamiliar. I then began to remember what he had taught at his last seminar in Dallas. *We have to feel safe whenever we are in unfamiliar situations, because our ego needs to have familiarity.* That thought helped put my mind at ease. I couldn't wait to learn more of what he taught.

I arrived at the training thirty minutes before it started. My friend dropped me off and I raced in to see if I could find Patrick before he got started. This was a large hotel and I had to stop and ask for help. The seminar was on the second floor in one of their special training rooms. There were two tables that were set up just the same way as he had it in Dallas. There were already many people there waiting to sign in and find a place in the room to sit. I looked around and didn't see him anywhere. As I approached the table to sign in and to get my name tag, I casually asked where Patrick was. The women said that he would be down in about twenty minutes and that I could go in and find a seat.

I was way too nervous to sit down. I paced the halls outside of the training room, while many people were coming up to get signed in. I was just waiting till the moment would arrive that I could look into those deep, beautiful, spiritual eyes. So many emotions were stirring deep within. I was really happy that we didn't have to go inside to wait. The walking, or shall I say pacing franticly up and down the hallways, seemed to settle my nerves. I paced so much I thought I would wear out the carpet. I noticed that many of the people were starting to go inside. Twenty minutes had passed by now and still no sign from Patrick. I wanted to be the first one to approach him. I wanted to wrap my arms tightly around him and never let him go. I also knew he had to teach and that I would have to play it really cool. I was curious how he would react when he saw me. I hoped that he would let me know in some secret way how happy he was to see me too.

Most everyone had already gone inside to find a seat. Right as I arrived at the door, I turned and saw him walking down the hall. He was smiling at me, looking right into my eyes. Without any hesitation, he came right over and gave me the biggest, warmest, most heartfelt hug ever! I lit up like a candlestick.

"Donza, I'm so happy to see you," he whispered. "We are going to have a lot of fun together."

My heart was elated. My ego flew out of my head. I was the first person that he came up to and the very first one that he hugged. I felt so special. He had such a way of making me feel important and cared for. All of the feelings that I had from the first time I ever saw him came flooding back into my body. It was such a delight to be filled with that kind of love and joy.

As he walked into the room, everyone stood up and began clapping for him. It was like he was a celebrity—some special kind of rock star status he had on the people in Los Angeles. I was very impressed. We all took our seats. I planted myself in the front row again. This time I was at the end of the row, because all the seats had already been taken. I was okay with sitting on the end. I thought it might be too distracting sitting in the center of the front row.

This seminar was about learning body language, reading faces, eyes, bodies and the fine details that separated those many distinctions. We were also going to get to work on people's bodies and tell them what we knew about them from their body language. It was all very new information and it seemed as though it was going to be a lot to learn and take in. We only had two days of training. Patrick had such a calming voice when he spoke. He made us all feel like it was going to be really easy to learn and that we all would be able to do it by the time we were finished. He had a way of encouraging that made me believe that we all would learn this new information fast and very well.

Within two days I learned how to tell if people were lying just by watching their eyes and how to know if you should trust people or not. There were many useful skills he taught, and we all practiced on each other several times to make sure we understood all the different meanings to our body language. He divided us into groups of four. Then he came by each group and tested us to see if we were reading the body correctly. This was easy to me. It just came naturally, as if I knew this information before, even though I didn't. Patrick was impressed. I felt proud that I was able to read the body parts he wanted me to.

"Great job, Donza," he would say. He flirted with me throughout the day.

* * *

It was nearing the end of the first day of training and I really wanted to spend time with him. I wasn't sure how to approach him. On one of the breaks I went up to him and asked what he was doing later.

He whispered, "I'm staying at this hotel, so why don't you

meet me for dinner later?"

I was so happy that we would be getting together. I had to play it cool, though. I couldn't wait to kiss him again and just be close to him in that intimate special way that only we would share.

As the training was finishing up for the first day, I was flying high knowing soon I would be in his arms again. So many people wanted his attention and he stayed to help everyone there. He made sure we all knew his techniques and could read body posture, hand gestures, and eye patterns. This was the most amazing information I had ever learned. There was still much more to know. I couldn't wait to learn it all.

Patrick came over to my group and told me to follow him to the front. He had to tell me something. He leaned in and, speaking in a very soft voice, told me to meet him downstairs in about an hour after the training. He stared into my eyes with the knowingness that we had this special connection that no one else shared. I felt like my heart was going to burst into flames at any given moment.

After the seminar was over I decided to walk around for a while. I had an hour to kill and I didn't want anyone there from the training knowing our business. He was very private and did not talk about his personal life often with others. I really respected that, and he was one of those men who really respected women too. He never talked badly about anyone ever. I went into the bathroom to freshen up. I wanted to look as good as possible for him. As I stood in front of the mirror there were two women in the bathroom that were from the training. I searched my purse as if I were looking for my lipstick. They were talking about how sexy and good looking Patrick was and that they couldn't wait to come back the next day. I smiled and didn't say a word. I felt very proud to say the least.

Chapter Fifteen

It was now time to meet him in the hotel restaurant. I had butter-flies twirling around inside my stomach. I walked up to the front door in the lobby and spotted him. He smiled at me as he reached his arms out to give me a hug. He squeezed me and started kissing my neck.

"You feel amazing!" he said as he wrapped me up in his arms and caressed my back. We stood there for several minutes enjoy-ing one another, and never once did we stop smiling. That he was happy and excited to see me was more than I had expected. I was still a little reserved and not as self-expressed as I wanted to be. Maybe it was because we were in public, or maybe it was that I was overwhelmed by his response to me. I knew that it was only a mat-ter of time before I would let go completely and start to be more of myself. I mean, I had been stripped down on every level with him. It was time now that I started expressing all of me to him. I was still just a little reluctant and that was okay.

We had an incredible dinner together and he shared many of the feelings that he was having about me. He was starting to fall for me. I sat there in complete awe. He was so open and honest about his feelings. He would stare right into my eyes. His warmth and love kept pouring out of them. It was hard to contain my passion for him. I told him that we needed to go up to his room very soon. He agreed.

Up to the room we went for another night of life-altering, mind-blowing passion. This time was more hot and heavy than the first time. I felt much more comfortable with him. I wasn't as shy or self-conscious. He was so intense in a way I had not felt before. He was letting himself go deeper than before. Our bodies were in perfect harmony with one another. It was like a spiritual dance. Merging together in this deep intimate way was such a beautiful thing. The connection we shared was priceless and he was the only man I ever wanted.

Our bodies were vibrating so much that it felt like we were going to transcend at any given moment. We began to synchronize our breathing and that seemed to intensify every feeling we were experiencing. I could feel his energy going to the core of my being, opening up my heart and soul. It was profound. I allowed myself to finally surrender to him fully.

The one thing about Patrick that I had noticed was that he was always consistent in his words and behaviors. He was never moody, angry, or sad about anything. He had such a positive outlook on life and felt grateful to be alive. He was so refreshing to be around. I hoped that one day I could be more like him.

After several hours with him, I knew that I couldn't stay the night. He had to be up early and do the second day of the training. I would be leaving him once again. I wasn't sad or disappointed at all. I would be seeing him tomorrow and have one more day with him. I was thrilled about that. As I was leaving, Patrick asked if I could come back and stay tomorrow night.

I answered with glee, "Yes!" I told him that my friend would be picking me up soon and that I couldn't wait to see him in the morning. We had one final molten-hot, good-bye kiss at the door.

My body was still vibrating and I wasn't fully in there yet. He embraced me tenderly and offered to walk me down.

"No, thank you." I didn't want to risk anyone from the training seeing us together. There were many people staying at the hotel, and I wanted to make sure no one knew about us. I left his room feeling elated and in love.

Chapter Sixteen

The next day I popped out of bed wide awake and ready to go. I arrived thirty minutes early at the hotel. I wondered what kind of a day was in store for us. This day I decided that I would go in first to find my seat and sit front-row center. As I walked in not expecting to see Patrick yet, I saw him standing in front of the class getting his mic gear sorted out. He turned around immediately and saw me walking toward him. He put his gear down and headed my way with arms stretched wide open. There were only a few people in the room. I dropped my things down on the nearest chair and was ready to greet my sweet love.

This time as we hugged he kept rocking back and forth, making this lovely sound of pleasure with each movement. "Mmmm, Mmmm . . ."

I was melting once again in his arms, taking all of him in with each breath.

"Meet me after the training," he whispered. This was going to be my last night in Los Angeles. Also, the last time I would see him for a while. I wasn't sure when we would be together again. I didn't want to think about that right now. I was being in the moment and enjoying every second of him.

I ventured off to find my seat. I had such a warm, cozy feeling bubbling up inside my chest. I was excited to learn more and be in his presence for the whole day and evening. I couldn't stop wondering if the entire class could feel our chemistry and attraction for one another. It was really hard to contain my feelings for him. I wanted to stand on the rooftop of the hotel and shout out, "I'm in love! I'm in love! For the first time ever in my life!" I wanted the world to know.

It was now time for the training to start. We all looked alert and refreshed. There was excitement circulating around the room.

Patrick began doing an overview of what we learned the day before and then started sharing with us all the many things that we were going to learn this final day. Today we would find a partner and work one-on-one with them, getting more into the detail of how to read the many different signals the body gives us. He told us that the body never lies and that it is our words and language that will. Today we would learn how to catch people in lies by how their bodies associated or disassociated and how they were congruent or incongruent with their words, posture, or body movements. It was all fascinating.

Patrick then asked for a volunteer. He brought a man up in front of the class so that he could read his body language and show us how he did it. Patrick asked many different questions and began to quickly read and interpret what he saw. It was the most extraordinary thing I had ever witnessed. He then started to reveal several things about the man's beliefs, values, and how he had a lot of negative self-talk always running in his head. The man stood there stunned. We all were. Patrick made it look easy and effortless. He then told us to pay very close attention to someone's breathing. It is very important to be able to watch and calibrate the speed, shallowness, or deep breaths that people do under different feelings they are having. It all means something. He then explained the meaning behind the breaths and how we would have to practice and pay attention more to become better and better. We then got with our partners and practiced calibrating body language. Again, Patrick walked around to each group and helped us individually, making sure we were listening to our intuition, reading and understanding all of the different signals the body was expressing.

I really enjoyed this part of the training the most. It was much better to be one-on-one with your partner in this kind of intimate, healing environment. Also, it was really great to have Patrick come over and spend time with each of us. This was totally a different kind of seminar than the one in Dallas. This time he wasn't standing in front of the room all day teaching. It was a hands-on approach with much more information and personal time with him. Not only did I prefer this, I seemed to learn much faster, and it was easier to take in all of the many modalities this way.

The day flew by. We took turns working on each other's body and then getting feedback from Patrick. It was such powerful information and I knew that I would be using all of the many skills and tools in my practice as a professional massage therapist and in my personal life, as well. On each break we would look for a new partner. By the end of the day we had practiced on many different people. My confidence had grown within just a few hours. Everyone was feeling more at ease and comfortable with this new information. It was all coming together now and we had learned so much in two days.

It was time now for the training to end. Patrick received another standing ovation for his brilliant training. The energy was high in the room and he was much more popular in his own town for sure. I knew it would be awhile before he was finished, because he had to talk to many people after the seminar. I went up to thank him casually and to receive my hug.

"I'll meet you at your room in an hour," I whispered.

"Perfect," he quietly replied back in my ear.

I felt special that I was the one getting to spend time with him alone. I was now realizing that this was going to be our last night together, for who knew how long? I could feel myself starting to get a little anxious about it. My feelings had grown much more for him over this weekend. I began to wonder how long I could actually do a long-distance relationship. Especially with a man who traveled all over the world and met many women along his journey. I also knew that tonight would be the night to open up my heart and tell him that I was falling in love. I was praying that he would be telling me those exact words, as well.

After an hour of walking around, a question kept going through my mind a thousand times: how was I going to have the courage to tell him how I really felt? An overwhelming fear took over my body, and I began to wonder what I would do if he rejected me and didn't feel the same.

Was I willing to risk it all?

Yes, I was.

I decided that it was time to stop living this fearful, small life that had kept me alone and single for so long. It was now time to follow my heart, for the first time listen and trust it most of all. No matter what the outcome, I would at least know that I would have no regrets as long as I stayed open and told him what I was feeling deep in my soul. I also knew he would always be kind and gentle even if he didn't want to go any further into this relationship. This was the longest hour that I ever had to endure.

I finally headed up toward his room. I walked over to the elevators and found him standing there, waiting for the doors to open. He was already looking at me.

"Hello," he said in a soft, sexy voice.

"Hi there!"

We stepped into the empty elevator. After the doors closed, he pushed me back against the mirrored wall and planted this deep, passionate, full-on kiss. It was like a scene from a movie. I had never been kissed like that before! The chemistry was almost overwhelming. The sexual desires I felt for him were completely overpowering. We were stepping into the Twilight Zone together and had just lost ourselves in that beautiful, exquisite moment of time. We couldn't keep our hands off each other as we walked down the hall to his room. Before he could open the door I was unbuttoning his shirt. I know it surprised him. I even shocked myself. I knew what I wanted and I wasn't holding back anymore. Patrick had unleashed this burning desire that had been hidden and locked away for years and now I was finally the one holding the key to my own sexual identity. It was all very natural as I awakened to a whole new level of liberation and sexual expression. I felt free to be myself and safe to allow him to see me as this sensual, sexy woman that had fully emerged.

We had another magical night together. Two souls connecting deeper each time we shared ourselves. I could now lose myself in this energy of passion, desire, and love. A feeling I had longed for my entire life. It was now happening to me, better than any dream I could have imagined. This was a true love story that was unfolding in divine order.

Patrick embraced my newfound freedom and really enjoyed watching me be so uninhibited. He knew the work that it had taken to get to this place. It was his healing, passion, and unconditional love that became my compass that guided me to a place of security and safety. His love was the healing ingredient for my soul.

This was the night to let him see into my heart, even though I knew he already was aware of my feelings. I felt like I had to actually say the spoken words in order for him to fully understand the depth of my love for him. I was lying across his chest, still trembling from the intensity that we had just shared, still feeling connected to him.

I whispered softly near his ear, "You are the most incredible man I have ever met in my life and I have never let go with anyone like this before. What I'm feeling is so deep and I'm really scared to share it all with you."

He held me tight in his arms and then leaned down to kiss me again. He turned his lips to my ear and whispered, "I love you." His words draped over my entire body, covering me like a warm security blanket. I felt tears starting to well up inside. I knew I had to say it back before I started gushing.

"I love you too!"

He gently pulled me over so I was now lying on top of him. "You never have to be afraid to share anything with me. You are so special and I really care about you."

By this time tears were streaming down my face. He knew that I didn't like to cry or show any emotions, but there was no way I could hold them back. He kept holding me and stroking my face as he wiped my tears away. There was nothing else we had to say in that moment. I sank down deeper across his chest. I had this overwhelming feeling of love and complete oneness with him. My prayers had been answered and all of my dreams had come true. I'd found my soul mate, and I felt as though the void inside had been filled.

Chapter Seventeen

After enjoying our time together we were ready for dinner. We decided to order room service again. I wanted to be alone with him with no distractions, and he was feeling the same. As the food arrived, we were sitting at this cozy, little table in the living room of his suite. I wanted to know more about his life and the many open stories that he never finished telling me. I began by asking, "Why don't you like talking on the phone? I love talking on the phone."

Patrick said, "When I was a little boy around eight years old, I woke up early in the morning to a light that was in the right corner of my room. I then heard my uncle's voice telling me to tell my father that my uncle was gone and that he was okay. When I went in to tell my dad what had happened, he said, 'What are you talking about? My brother went into the hospital for a hernia operation. It was a very minor surgery. Go back to bed.' Within ten minutes the phone rang and it was the hospital telling my father that his brother had just passed away from complications. He started yelling and screaming, then wouldn't look or talk to me for weeks. He thought I was some kind of freak. Ever since then I associated the phone with my father and all the yelling, screaming, and negative things I had been told."

It was an incredible story to hear him tell. I could still feel the upset in his voice when he talked about it. "I am not as bad about the phone as I use to be. I would much rather communicate in person. I also had a terrible speech impediment when I was a child. I would mumble my words and speak very softly, so it was very difficult to understand what I was saying. I was also extremely shy and wouldn't look at anyone when I spoke. There were many obstacles that I had to overcome as a young child."

It was hard to believe that he used to have all of those problems. It was also incredible that he had overcome so much. Now he was a communication-and-body-language expert, leading seminars around the world and teaching some of the most profound healing information I had ever heard.

"You are the most amazing man I have ever met. I am blown away by your stories. You have to write a book about your life."

He smiled. "Thank you. I'm planning to do that one day."

"I have one more thing to ask you . . . What the hell were those silver sparkles that came out of your nose?"

He reached over to hold my hands. "I'm not going to share that with you right now."

I was so disappointed. I wanted to know now more than ever.

"You're not going to tell me?"

"No, not right now." He picked up my hand and kissed it ever so sweetly. "I will tell you at some point. I promise."

Although I was really curious, I decided not to push the subject anymore.

We sat there finishing up our meal and I was grateful to have one more night with him. He was going to be traveling all over for the next month and wasn't coming back to Dallas anytime soon.

"When will I see you again?" I asked.

"I'm not sure. I will call you . . . I promise."

"When will you call me?" I needed to know so that I wouldn't be waiting by the phone or wondering when or if.

"I will call you after my trainings on a Monday or Tuesday. I will give you the number where I will be staying that week so you can call me if you'd like."

I felt a little relieved. This showed that he really wanted to talk and that he did care. I also knew now what a big deal it was for him about the phone. As I started to say thank you, he pulled my hand up with his and we both were now standing.

"Thank you," I whispered in his ear.

He started kissing me again with such a tenderness and passion that was always present between us. Once again I was in his loving arms and enjoying every moment of him. I wished that I didn't have to leave the next day. We shared another intimate night wrapped so closely that we could feel each other's hearts beating together as one. It was the most spiritual and beautiful feeling to have this kind of connection with another soul, especially the man I was in love with. I felt loved and free to allow myself to go deep inside of those feelings of unconditional love.

Chapter Eighteen

The next morning arrived. I had the whole morning to be with him until my flight to Dallas. This day was going to be especially hard for me because this time I wasn't sure when we would see each other again. It was too difficult to even allow myself to think about it. I wanted our last few hours together to be perfect without my insecurities creeping up or my incessant fears taking over; even though I knew he would feel them anyway and probably would want to discuss them. I needed at this time to keep them to myself. I noticed that Patrick too was quieter this morning, and I could feel that he had a lot on his mind. I wondered if he was feeling or thinking about some of the same things I was. We had taken this relationship to a whole new level and depth. We had said the three magic words that seem to imply that we were now together, a real couple.

As we ate breakfast, he held my hand and asked, "How are you feeling?"

"I am so grateful that I met you and that we were able to share this special time together. I just don't want it to be over today."

"It's not going to be over today. This is just the beginning."

I had been worried about so many things, that I didn't even

realize this was just the beginning. That was exactly what I needed to hear to calm my fears down and ease my anxious mind.

"When do you think we will see each other again?" I asked. I could still feel many insecurities stirring inside. I had never been in a long-distance relationship before, nor had I ever really been in love either. This was a whole new experience that I was delving deep down into head first. I must say that I was very apprehensive and a little uneasy in the beginning. I also knew that I had to trust him more and, most of all, trust myself. Listening to my intuition and following my heart were the only things that I knew how to do. I was going to have to take a leap of faith and not only trust, but believe that what was happening at this point in my life was the most profound and significant thing that I had ever experienced.

"I'm not sure when we will see each other," he said. "What I do know is that I will call you whenever I can and that I will be thinking of you often. I will come to you in your dreams."

I sighed and, squeezing his hand, leaned over and kissed him. Once again tears welled up inside, though these tears were different than before. These were happy tears. For the first time I felt that he was falling in love with me too. It was incredible to be falling in love, and to feel the love being given back was the most extraordinary feeling.

Patrick said, "Let's have some fun today."

"What do you have in mind?"

"I want to take you shopping before you have to leave."

"Really! I would love to! Where do you want to go?"

"Have you ever been to Rodeo Drive in Beverly Hills?"

"No, never!"

We finished our breakfast, got dressed, and we were both ready to go in no time. He also told me that he would be taking me to the airport. This was a complete surprise. I was planning on taking a shuttle because my friend had to work.

He said, "We will stop by your friend's place to collect your bags and then go shopping." He had it all planned out. I really loved that he was taking charge and, most of all, spending quality time with me. I had so much energy and enthusiasm at this point that I could hardly contain myself.

We left the hotel holding hands, walking side by side. Finally we didn't have to hide anything or keep it a secret anymore. *This must be what heaven feels like.* Feeling intimacy and unconditional love with another soul was what life was all about. All of the love stories and fairy tales that I had grown up with could never penetrate my skepticism or my carefully protected heart. That now had all changed. My heart had finally opened and I allowed the most incredibly loving, caring, spiritual man to go deep inside. I don't think I could have done anything to stop it.

He was The One.

* * *

Our first stop was to go get my luggage and leave a note for my friend to thank her for everything. I was hoping that she could have met Patrick at this time, but she had already left for work. We loaded my bags into his car and now we were off to Beverly Hills to go shopping together. I was thrilled. He had all of these places that he wanted to take me. I could plainly see that he was excited too. He parked his car in this underground parking lot. He then leaned over and gazed into my eyes and said, "You're going to have a lot of fun today." Then he started kissing me passionately again. Sparks ran up and down my spine. That was the perfect way to start our shopping adventure together.

He took me to every designer store and kept asking me what I wanted. He offered to buy me anything that my heart desired. I didn't want anything except to be spending time with him. I never had a man that was so generous, nor had I ever spent very much time in these kinds of exclusive, expensive stores before. I was definitely feeling out of my element for sure. We had an absolute blast walking around Beverly Hills together, hand in hand. He really enjoyed showing me all of his favorite designer stores: Armani, Gucci, Halston, different restaurants and art galleries too. He kept telling me to pick something out that I wanted. But I just couldn't. I didn't feel comfortable with him buying me anything at this point in our relationship, especially from these expensive stores. I wasn't one to spend that kind of money on designer anything. Although I was grateful that he wanted to pamper me, I wouldn't let him buy me anything. He had very expensive taste for sure. He showed me some of the Armani suits that he had just bought. They were beautiful.

"You must look amazing in those suits, I'm sure," I said.

He smiled and kissed my cheek.

We walked for almost two hours. I had never gone shopping with a man for that long before. He was definitely like no other man I knew.

How many men like to do this? I wondered.

I was feeling blessed to be here spending time with him and really getting to know more about him. I loved every minute of it. He wanted to sit down at a coffee shop and get something to drink. We didn't have much time left before I was to head off to the airport. As we sat down I could feel some anxiety coming up about leaving him and about flying.

Right when I started to think it, he asked, "How are you feeling?"

I took a deep breath and began to tell him, which was such progress that I was able to express to him right away what I was feeling. "I feel sad that I have to go and I wish that I had more time with you." I also confessed about my intense fear of flying.

He reached his hands across the table and held mine. He stared straight into my eyes and said in such a calm and comforting voice, "You don't have to worry about flying. Everything is going to be all right. I wish you didn't have to go back so soon." He picked my hands up and kissed them ever so gently. His tender words released my worries and fears and put me at ease. I trusted his intuition. He had been right every time thus far.

We were only sitting for a few minutes when he pulled something out of his pocket. It was a piece of jade, about four inches long, and two inches wide.

"I want you to keep this with you," Patrick said. "This will protect you and give you healing in times of sadness or fear." He gently placed it in my hand. It felt warm and I could feel a slight pulse coming from it. "Can you feel the energy?" he asked.

"I've never felt energy come off a piece of a stone before."

"This is a very powerful stone. Promise me that you will keep this with you wherever you go."

"Yes, I promise. Thank you so much!" I could feel how special this stone was to him. I felt honored and truly blessed that he had given it to me.

Our next stop was LAX. I wasn't ready to leave him yet. I could feel he was having difficultly too. We held hands the entire drive there.

"I had so much fun shopping with you," I said. "I really appreciate that you made time for me."

He began asking questions again about how I was feeling. I was very honest about feeling sad and afraid of how much I was going to miss him. Also, how it really bothered me that we had no idea when we would see each other again.

"How are *you* feeling?" I asked.

"Like we will see each other very soon." He squeezed my hand to signal that he believed what he was saying.

I felt very comforted and relieved.

He parked his car at the airport and offered to walk me to my gate. What a great surprise! I thought that he would just be dropping me off, the same way that I did with him. He really wanted to spend this time together. I could feel how much more attached he was getting now. We checked my bags curbside and proceeded to go through security. He was going to wait until I got on the plane before he left. I felt relieved and my fear of flying dissipated. We sat next to one another with his arms wrapped around my shoulders, hugging and stroking my back. I snuggled my face up in to his neck and kept breathing in his delicious smell. Being held in his arms and feeling his essence was the peace and comfort I needed before this flight. He wasn't shy about showing affection in public and for the first time, neither was I. We didn't talk very much at this time. We just enjoyed the sweetness of these moments together. It was now time to board the flight. As we stood up I fell into his arms. I didn't know how I was ever going to let him go. We started kissing one final passionate, love-filled kiss that completely swept me off my feet. My heart was full and I felt close and connected to him.

"I love you," he whispered in my ear.

"I love you too!" Once again the tears started falling. For someone who didn't cry often I was now leaking all over the place.

Patrick smiled. "I will call you tonight." As he walked me to the gate, I was the last person to board. I handed my ticket to the flight attendant. Patrick was able to stand there and watch as I went through the corridors. We never said good-bye. I turned one final time and blew him a kiss. I will never forget the loving expression he had on his face. He looked so beautiful and his spirit was bright. He blew a kiss back and then gave me his sexy wink that I always loved.

I walked the rest of the way down the tunnel with tears streaming down my face. I quickly reached for my sunglasses and placed them over my crying eyes. I boarded the plane and took my seat, sank down in my chair, and kept my sunglasses on the entire flight. Every thought was consumed with him and our time together. I wasn't feeling fear at all about flying. I pulled out the piece of jade from my purse and held it close to my heart.

Chapter Nineteen

I landed back in Dallas safe and sound, still feeling his presence all around me. I could hardly wait for his phone call. I unpacked and did everything I could possibly do to keep myself busy until he called. Finally, at ten o'clock the phone rang and it was him. We talked for such a long time. I thanked him over and over, telling him what a great time I had. He kept telling me that I was very special to him and that he was excited to share such quality time together. We just weren't sure when we would see each other again. Although this time I wasn't worried at all. I felt him wanting us to be together just as much as I did. He was very sweet and had many positive things to say about our time together and all of the many things he was feeling. He ended the conversation telling me that he loved me and was missing me already.

"I love you, too," I replied.

He then promised that he would call from every place he would be traveling to and how long he would be there. It was exactly what I needed to hear to help me feel secure about our long-distance relationship.

Sure enough, by the end of the next weekend Patrick called from another city. He was on the East Coast doing trainings and private sessions. He was working twelve to fourteen hours a day and planned to be there for at least a week. He still had a two-day seminar that he was going to be giving. I could hear in his voice how tired and drained he was.

"Patrick, please get some rest and take care of yourself."

"I really love what I do, so it doesn't feel like I'm working."

Nevertheless, I was concerned, though I knew that he was used to working long hours.

I said, "I really care about you and want you to be well."

"Thank you. You do not have to worry." But of course I still did.

This became my life, waiting each week to hear from him by phone. He worked more than anyone I had ever known and traveled all over the United States, filling up his seminars and private sessions. The word was out and he was in much demand. People would fly in all over the country just to see Patrick. The healing work that he did was like no other at this time. His talents and many gifts were being talked about all over the world now. I was proud of him and his work. I knew the positive impact he was making on many people's lives, and I was sure that soon he would be well known and perhaps even famous. No one else did what he could do. He was truly unique.

I could hardly wait for him to return to Dallas.

* * *

Weeks turned into months.

I was still getting my weekly phone calls and missing him terribly by this time. Still not knowing when we would see each other, I was feeling restless and sad. It had been almost three months since I had seen him. He was back on the West Coast working away. I got a call from him at the beginning of the week which was unusual. He normally called on Sunday nights after his seminar. It was a nice surprise.

"Hi there!" I said. "Is everything all right?"

"Yes, everything's fine. I have great news. I will be in Dallas in three weeks!"

"What! Are you serious?" I was now squealing over the phone. "I'm so excited to see you!"

"I am too! I will be there for four days. Two days of private sessions and two days of training. You can tell everyone you know that I will be there. Also, I would really love it if you would help coordinate my seminar for me. Get as many people as you can to attend."

I was thrilled! I knew that I could get a lot of people to his training and that he would keep busy while he was here. I also planned to finally spend some much-needed quality time with him.

"I'm looking forward to seeing you, Patrick."

"I will be kissing your sexy lips soon. I can hardly wait!"

A surge of sexual energy shot through my body. I wasn't shy about expressing my feelings with him anymore. I told him exactly what I was feeling and he, too, was feeling the same way. Only three weeks until I was to be with the love of my life again.

As I hung up I reached for my phone book. I was going call everyone I knew to tell them the good news. I had not told many people about our relationship. I knew that he would be back in Dallas and I didn't want to compromise his privacy, nor have people think that I would be getting any special treatment in his seminars. Even though I knew I would. Three weeks was the perfect amount of time to let everyone know that he was coming to town.

Patrick had two other coordinators here in Dallas. I was able to connect with them and let them know I was going to help spread the word. They didn't know about our relationship, and Patrick wanted to keep it that way. It was going to be difficult to contain my feelings for him so that the coordinators would not suspect anything. I had to remain professional and do whatever I could to support him while he was in Dallas.

* * *

The three weeks flew by fast. Thank God!

Many people had confirmed that they would be attending Patrick's seminar and that they were very excited to meet him. I had tons of energy and enthusiasm when I spoke of Patrick. I'm sure it was plain to see that I was attracted to him. There was a part of me that wanted to tell everyone I knew that I was in love with the most incredible man ever! I had to respect his feelings about it, so I didn't tell anyone we were dating. It was the appropriate thing to do since I was now helping coordinate it.

Patrick arrived on a Wednesday evening. He was staying at the same hotel as the last time he was in town. He was going to be doing private sessions on Thursday and Friday, then the seminar Saturday and Sunday. He asked if I wanted to pick him up from the airport and have dinner with him. Of course the answer was yes! He had to meet up later that night with his two other coordinators. They were a married couple and had been dear friends of Patrick for years. I wondered if I was going to be able to spend the night with him. He assured me that we would definitely have some intimate time together while he was here.

When I arrived at the airport I was nervous and excited to see him again. I waited by the gate impatiently, hoping that he would be the first one off the plane and that I would be the first person he saw when he walked through that gate.

The plane was on time and people started walking out the door. He wasn't the first one off, but it didn't take long before I saw this tall, handsome, beautiful man walking toward me with the biggest smile across his face. He dropped his bag and I ran into his wide open arms, hugging and squeezing his neck. He picked me up off my feet and twirled me around. We kissed intensely right there in the terminal. I felt totally lost in that moment. Waves of pleasure surged through my entire body, as though I was being touched by him for the very first time. It was such an overwhelming feeling of love, passion, and divine spirit entering into my being. We were so deeply connected with one another that I almost forgot that we were still standing at the gate. I kept thinking, *I am so in love with this man.* The words rang throughout my head over and over like church bells. *Thank you, God, for sending this love to my life.*

We collected his luggage and I drove us back to the hotel. He only had a short time before he was meeting with his Dallas co-ordinators. We checked into the hotel, skipped dinner, and went straight up to his room. We shared another beautiful evening. He had a way of being that always felt alive and childlike at the same time. He was very playful and had an abundance of energy. It was truly magical spending this special time with one another. Each intimate time we shared together felt like we were delving down deeper into each other's souls.

* * *

It was now time for him to get ready to meet his friends that were helping with the seminar. I told him that I had thirty to forty people coming to his weekend training.

He looked totally stunned. "Are you serious?"

"Yes, completely serious."

"Thank you so much!" He was surprised because the last time he was here there were only about fifty people total. Now I was bringing a whole lot more. He said, "You need to be here with us tonight. Let me call them and let them know how many people you're bringing."

"Sure, I would love to stay."

"After they leave can you stay the night?" he asked.

"I didn't bring any extra clothes because I didn't know that I would be staying over."

"You don't need anything, Donza. If you do we can go buy it."

I was hoping that I could contain myself around his friends. I had to put on my professional hat and act like I was just another one of Patrick's groupies and wanted to contribute as much as possible. This was going to be the hardest thing to do ever. We were both radiating all of this sexual energy and attraction toward each other. How in the world were we going to not show it in front of his friends?

Chapter Twenty

Later that evening we met up with his friends in the hotel lobby. I went down first and pretended to be just arriving. Patrick waited for a while before he came down. I greeted his friends and told them how nice it was to see them again as we all waited for him to meet us. When Patrick arrived he looked laid back and relaxed. You would have never suspected anything.

He hugged us all and we sat down, ready to discuss his weekend schedule and to get all the details needed so I could assist in this process. His coordinators only had twenty-five people confirmed thus far. I had at least thirty confirmed and probably more. Patrick was clearly impressed that I was enrolling more people than his two friends. He said that his goal was to have seventy-five or more for the weekend. We only had two more days to go before the training. I knew that I would do whatever it took to spread the word about his work. I, too, would be participating in the training and doing some assisting, also learning everything he was teaching.

We were in this meeting for over an hour. His friends wanted to go to the bar and order drinks. All I wanted was to go back up to his room and spend another passionate, romantic night. I didn't drink at all. I told them that I would talk to them later, really meaning Patrick. I knew he had a lot of catching up to do with his friends. They all insisted that I stay. Of course I wanted to be near him, though I didn't know how long I could keep up this professional front.

Patrick started telling them that I was one of the best body workers he ever had before. He kept complimenting me and I got really embarrassed. *What is he doing?* He was going to be the one blowing our cover. I suppose they knew how he was with the compliments, because he was also saying very kind words to his friends.

We stayed for two more hours and I watched them order drinks. We did have some appetizers, which I was thrilled since we had skipped dinner. They made plans to pick Patrick up in the morning to take him to his private appointments. He was going to be doing them in the same office building where he had done his incredible, life-transforming, healing work on me. He had twelve hours booked for both days already. He was in much demand here in Dallas. I really hoped that we would have a lot of people show up for his weekend seminar. He was starting at ten in the morning. I was now becoming anxious about the time. It was getting late and I knew that if we didn't wrap this up soon then I wasn't going to be staying the night.

He then looked in my eyes and said, "I think it's about time I head on up to my room."

I wasn't sure how to handle it, so I just played along. "Yes, it's getting late."

We all stood up and gave each other hugs good-bye. Patrick squeezed my arm to give me the signal that he wanted me to come back. I played it very cool and actually walked out with his friends to act like I was getting my car. Thank God they didn't valet. After they left the hotel, I ran as fast as I could back to Patrick's room.

He opened the door and was absolutely glowing. He looked like the Cheshire cat grinning from ear to ear like we had just gotten away with something. I leaped into his arms as if we had just started the evening all over again. We had a wild, romantic night that lasted for hours. We couldn't get enough of each other. Every precious moment I shared with him was the oxygen I needed to breathe. His presence and energy invigorated my mind, body, and spirit. This euphoria was a feeling I could get used to everyday. The more time we spent together the deeper these feelings grew. It was now time to let him know just how deeply I was falling for him. Although I was a little apprehensive about telling him, I knew that I couldn't hold back anything anymore. I mean, we had already told each other how much we loved one another. I needed to say more so that he could really feel the impact he had made on my life. As I laid my head against his chest, I was feeling completely relaxed and at home in his arms. With each breath I took, my heart filled with more love for him.

I said, "I care so much about you and feel a little scared about my feelings toward you. I need you in a way that I never needed anyone before. I don't want to come across as this needy, insecure, naïve girl that keeps gushing all over the place."

He whispered, "Donza, I love it when you allow yourself to open up to feel and say the truth that's in your heart."

"Does this scare you how I feel?"

"No, not all. You are beautiful and precious. And I am proud of you for opening up your lovely heart to me. I love you and feel that we have a very deep connection that will always keep growing. You will always have a special place in my heart."

This was exactly what I needed to hear. I never knew a man could express himself this freely and openly. I felt intoxicated once again by his ability to create a safe space that would help me feel even more loved and nurtured by him. I fell asleep in his warm, comforting arms that night and slept peacefully.

Chapter Twenty-one

We awoke early the next morning. I had to make sure I was gone before his friends came to pick him up. Patrick had to work two jam-packed days of private sessions. I wasn't sure if I would see him again before the seminar.

He said, "I will call you later when I'm finished."

I had a busy day myself with teaching and giving massages to my own clients. I was happy for the distractions. Knowing that my beloved was in my city and not getting to spend every minute with him was hard to handle. As I was getting dressed in the bathroom, Patrick came up from behind and wrapped his arms around me. I turned around and we started kissing again, our lips blazing. Kissing him had now become one of my favorite things in the world. We had to pull ourselves apart quickly or we both knew I would never get out of there on time.

He walked me down to the valet. "I will call you later." Then with a soft kiss, he said, "I love you."

I felt tingles spiral through my body again. The kind that stays present the whole day.

* * *

The two days Patrick was doing his private sessions seemed to drag by. Even though I knew that I would be seeing him at the seminar this weekend, I wanted our alone time together. I understood that he was here to work and that I needed to have more patience and understanding.

He called that night after his last session. He was back in his hotel room and sounded exhausted.

"Are you all right?" I asked.

"Yes, just a little tired."

I was hoping he would invite me to come over and stay the night, but I could tell he needed his rest. We kept the conversation brief and he said that he would call tomorrow.

Friday went by a little faster than the day before. I waited anxiously that night for his call. It was now around eleven o'clock and still no word from him yet. I crawled into bed wondering if I should call the hotel and see if he was there. I decided to give him a little more time. After all, he told me he would call. I needed to just wait which was always hard to do. I wasn't the most patient person when it came to waiting around for someone. It was getting close to midnight and I was about ready to call it a night when the phone finally rang.

"Hey, Donza, are you still awake?" Patrick asked.

"Yes, barely, how are you?"

"We all went to have a late dinner. That's why it's taken so long to call you."

"I was getting worried," I said.

"It's been a long day and I have another busy one tomorrow."

"Thank you for calling. You must be exhausted."

"Yes, I'm ready to sleep. I will miss you tonight."

"I will miss you too."

I was hoping that he would suggest that I come over tonight to stay with him, but I knew he was way too tired for that.

"I love you."

"I love you too!"

This was the briefest conversation that we had ever had. I didn't mind at all. I was so happy that he called even though he was tired. I didn't tell him about how many people I had enrolled in his seminar yet. I thought I would surprise him. I wanted him to be more rested before I gave him the good news. Starting tomorrow I would spend two days in his seminar, learning everything I could. I was excited to tell him that I had forty people coming. I knew that he would be very pleased about that.

*　*　*

I woke up early Saturday morning with such excitement and energy. Finally, the day had arrived that I was to be with him the whole day. I received a call from his coordinator asking if I could get there one hour before the seminar started. He needed help setting up the room and with registration. I was thrilled to be helping out and to be in his sacred inner circle. That would also mean that I would see Patrick a few minutes before the training started and hopefully have some alone time.

I arrived at the place where the seminar was being held. The two coordinators were there but Patrick was nowhere in sight. I wondered where he could be. "Where's Patrick?" I asked.

"He went to get coffee and finish preparing for the day."

My heart sank down into my chest. I wanted to see him without everyone around. You could plainly see my disappointment as I went into the training room and started setting up chairs. They gave me instructions of everything they needed help with. Within minutes of setting up the room I turned toward the door and discovered that Patrick had been standing there watching me. Smiling. I quickly finished what I was doing and rushed over to him.

We both reached our arms out and hugged.

He said, "I just heard how many people you have coming! You're incredible! I really appreciate all that you've done." He pulled me against his chest. He kept holding me in his arms and didn't seem to mind at all that his friends were around, which I was very happy about.

He whispered, "I want you to come to my hotel tomorrow night after the training if you can."

"Of course I can!" I had to contain myself and keep looking as professional as possible.

"It's hard not to kiss you right now," he said in a soft voice.

"I know."

He took a deep breath and made this sweet cooing sound as he gently stepped back from our embrace. Waves of joy washed my over my entire body. I wished that I could have shouted out to the whole room, "He's with me! We are in love!" But right now that wasn't going to happen. This was a seminar very much like the one he had done here before. I was looking forward to taking it again. I needed to learn and practice more of what he taught, learning how to have success and happiness without sabotaging it.

He began his day with seventy people in the training. I was proud of him and of myself for being able to contribute my time, energy, and love to help create an extraordinary turnout. I knew it was only a matter of time before his work and teachings would grow in Dallas even more than he could have imagined. I was going to make sure that I did everything I could to assist in that process.

For the next two days he took us through many of his healing processes and taught more about language, communication, and the importance of recognizing when we are in our egos. Once again much healing, breakthroughs, and emotional clearing were happening for us all. Patrick was able to create a space of safety and a feeling of deep connection with everyone in that room. It was magical to watch him work. He had such charisma and his powerful presence alone could change the energy in the room where you could feel the healing taking place. Everyone was impressed with him and the training was a huge success. He too was very pleased about the healings and connections he was making in Dallas.

At the end of the seminar, once again people stood up and clapped for him. The energy in the room was high, and Patrick took a humble bow. I stayed after everyone was leaving to assist with closing up the room and getting everything put back in place.

Patrick soon came over. "I will see you in about an hour."

I nodded. His coordinators were taking him to the hotel, so I had to play it cool. I still couldn't believe that no one knew our secret. Well, if they did they weren't letting on about it. I finished up everything and said my good-byes. Then I was off to spend another magical night of ecstasy.

Chapter Twenty-two

When I arrived at his hotel I was still flying high from all of the things he taught and shared. I could listen to him for hours and never be bored. He was an encyclopedia of information. I was fortunate to now have the opportunity to be alone with him. When I knocked on his door, he opened it quickly and pulled me inside. Before the door even closed we had already started kissing. We were like two love-crazed teenagers. We couldn't keep our hands off each other. This shy, insecure young woman had now fully awakened. I didn't quite recognize myself. It felt so right to be uninhibited.

We collapsed onto the bed, peeling each other's clothes off. We took our passion to another level—more intensity, deeper connection. That night we became a part of each other's souls. We intertwined, breathing as one, loving in such a deep, unconditional way that I knew that I would never be the same again. This love took me to places inside myself that I never knew existed. I wondered how much deeper could I go with this beautiful soul. I was living and breathing inside a place of love and spirituality with a sense of freedom from the everyday world. I listened to my heart and trusted my feelings when it came to expressing love with Patrick.

God had brought the perfect man to assist in my healing, growth, and, most of all, learning to love unconditionally. We spent hours together loving one another in such a close, intimate way. I had only read about this kind of intimacy in fairy tales. Now it was actually happening. I never wanted this night to end.

* * *

The next morning I woke up before him and crawled out of bed to go sit alone on the sofa. I was feeling sad that he was leaving. I wasn't sure how I would be able to say good-bye to him this time. I was ready to move to Los Angeles and announce to the world that we were together and in love. I just needed to be patient and wait for him to ask. His life was going full speed ahead and he was traveling all over the world. I would be away from him in L.A. too. I decided to continue on with this long-distance relationship and wait to see how it would all unfold. I wanted to be in the moment and not worry about anything. But I found it difficult to remain in the present not knowing when we would be together again.

Patrick came in and sat next to me. He could feel that I was processing a lot of mixed emotions. He wrapped his arms around me and held me close.

"What are we doing?" I whispered. "I don't know how long I can go without seeing you again. This is really hard and I'm not sure if I can do it for much longer."

"We will see each other soon. I promise. I will fly you out in the next few weeks."

That eased much of my sadness and worry just knowing that we would be seeing each other way sooner than before.

We spent the rest of the morning together in a very loving, passionate way.

I took him to the airport and told him that I couldn't say

good-bye.

"I will call you tonight," he said.

We held each other and there was so much love channeling through us. He kept kissing my lips over and over, soft, tender kisses as he held my face with his hands. It took everything inside of me not to break down into tears again. I just kept thinking to myself that I would be seeing him soon.

PART THREE
Two Souls Adrift

Chapter Twenty-three

For the next two and a half years our relationship didn't change much. We traveled back and forth, seeing each other whenever we had the chance. And then in the fall of 1990 the circumstances drastically altered between us.

Patrick was getting ready to travel around the world again for the second time since we had been together. I wasn't going to be traveling with him, because I was in school taking communication classes and he was too busy working. I had felt him pulling away and becoming distant over the past several months. I didn't know what to do. Patrick was going to be gone for nine months on this trip. We both knew there was no way I was going to be able to wait for him unless he was to propose, and I knew he wasn't ready for that. I started trying to prepare myself emotionally for that dreaded day that I knew was coming any minute now. How could I even imagine him not in my life anymore? I truly didn't know how I was going to handle it all. I knew that I couldn't take being second in his life anymore. I also knew how important his work and success were to him at this time in his life. I wanted him to be successful, and I believed in him and his work. I also believed in our love and wanted us to be together through it all. Unfortunately, he focused more on his career, not on love and staying connected through our long-distance relationship.

I will never forget the day that changed my life forever. It was September 5, 1990 and Patrick was in New York working. He called early that evening while I was eating dinner. He had such a loving, sweet tone to his voice. I was very surprised to hear from him this early.

"How are you?" he asked.

"Good." I felt this huge knot sink down to the pit of my stomach.

"I need to talk to you."

"I know," I murmured.

"Do you know that I really love you?"

"Yes," I whispered. I could feel the tears starting to well up in my eyes.

"You also know that I will be gone a long time on this trip. It's not fair for you to have to wait for me. I will always be here for you. What we have shared is rare and you are so special to me. I really need you to know that."

I was trying to hold off the tears and not break down and fall apart while on the phone with him.

"Do you understand?" he asked.

No, no! I don't understand! How can you choose work over love? I wanted to scream, but couldn't. He was being tender and loving and I could feel he knew how hard this was going to be for me. I became very quiet and let him continue talking and sharing his feelings. I never could have imagined that going through a breakup could be so kind and gentle. Most of all he was so loving and I could hear how much he cared in every word he spoke. He explained that he didn't want me to wait for him and that I deserved someone who I would be able to settle down with. Patrick wasn't ready for that. He had big dreams and was committed to his work, which he put all of his heart, passion, and love into. I knew that no matter what happened in my life we would always have this profound connection. And the depth of love I felt for him would forever remain deep inside my heart. The hardest thing about letting go was it was going to be very difficult for us both. We truly loved each other. I knew he never wanted to hurt my feelings or me to think he didn't love me in anymore. I always felt love from him, but how was I going to let the love of my life go and get through this?

I started breaking down. "I don't want to lose you. I want you in my life, Patrick. I'm willing to wait for you." Tears started falling down my cheeks. At this point I was feeling desperate. I had to say everything I was feeling. I knew I had to do anything to keep this relationship, or at least be open to any possibilities for us to stay together.

"We will always be connected," he said, his voice starting to crack. "Never think that you are losing me." He began crying along with me. I had never seen him cry nor had I heard him this emotional before. This was the most difficult thing to go through. I didn't know how to handle hearing him this way nor did I know what to say.

"I love you, Donza. I really love you," he kept saying. Those words washed over me like a crystal waterfall, clearing all of my doubts and fears. I felt that no matter what we would someday be together again. I had to believe this or I would have never been able to hang up the phone. What was difficult to understand was that we had never had any fights or disagreements that most couples would have had to get them to this breakup point. He was living an exciting fast-paced life. I knew I couldn't stand in his way. I didn't want him to stay in this relationship unless he was really ready to commit, which clearly he was not ready at all. Deep down, I wasn't ready either. Although at the time I surely didn't know it yet. As we were ending the call, Patrick told me to call him whenever I needed him and that he would always be there for me.

"Thank you," I said with tears streaming down my face. I didn't want to hang up.

He reassured me that we were going to get through this. "I love you very much," he whispered. He was also having a difficult time hanging up.

"Good-bye, Patrick. I love you. Thank you for everything you have given my life. I am so grateful to you. You have changed my life in such a deep profound way and I will never be the same. I am such a better person because of knowing and loving you."

"You're incredible and I love you. Never forget that. Do you hear me?"

"I love you always." I blew one final kiss into the phone and hung up. I couldn't really believe that I actually put down the receiver, but I did it. Every emotion came rushing out as I collapsed onto the floor, sobbing my guts out. I wasn't sure how I would make it through all of these feelings. Let alone have a life that didn't include him in it. I lay there wondering if I would ever get over him as I kept allowing all the tears and feelings to unleash.

I eventually got off the floor. I had to put my energy and focus into something else for a while or I would never be able to get through all of this. So that's what I did. I started getting involved with many different healing classes and communication courses. I started going to a new church called Unity. I was training more in the gym and working as much as possible, anything to help keep my mind off Patrick. I saw a therapist, hoping she would have some magic words to help ease my heavy, broken heart. Therapy helped a little, but nothing I did stopped my pain and longing for him. I felt as though I was going through the dark nights of my soul with no end in sight. No matter what I did or how hard I tried, I could not let him go. In fact, each night for months I cried myself to sleep. I lay in the darkness of my room, wondering what I could have done differently for us to have stayed together. These were the insidious thoughts that plagued my tortured mind and broken heart.

Chapter Twenty-four

After a year of no dating, some very intense therapy, and lots of inner work that I did on myself, I began to feel like I was coming back to the real world—a world in which I could possibly find love again. I chose not to be in contact with Patrick the whole year. It was the hardest thing I ever had to do. My therapist thought it would be like ripping the scab off the old wound and having it bleed all over the place if I were to be in contact with him and not be over him. I took her advice. I never heard from him. I'm sure he knew how difficult it would have been on me, so in some ways I was relieved and disappointed.

Nevertheless, I allowed myself to spend time healing and growing in this year of heartbreak. It was exactly what I needed to help get to a new level of understanding and clarity. I was able to see the many gifts his presence had in my life and the profound effect he made in my own work that I was doing with people. Most of all I cherished the impact and healing that was still occurring deep within myself, because I was now opening up my emotions and allowing myself to be more self-expressed. I owed so much to Patrick for this miraculous healing I was going through. He helped start my life on this spiritual journey as I traveled to the depths of my emotions through the many doorways of growth, evolution, and spiritual awareness. This was where the real awakenings occurred in my soul. I have had so much passion for learning, teaching, healing, and many different spiritual modalities. Anything that I could learn that would help heal someone's wounds and make a positive impact, I was doing it and it was all because of Patrick's influence in my life.

Chapter Twenty-five

Three years had passed now. I found out that he was going to be doing a new seminar, one he had never taught before. It was to be in Los Angeles, August of 1993. It was for two days only and I knew that I had to go. We did have a few conversations on the phone in the past two years. We kept it very light and simple. Each time we spoke I still felt the connection. He always said "I love you" at the end of each call. I knew that he meant it. I still loved him and it was now in a way that wasn't torturing. I could actually say good-bye without tears following the call. He had said we would always be friends, and I accepted the fact that a loving friendship was the most he could ever offer me.

I knew it was going to be difficult seeing him again. Yet I knew that I had to go. So I called his coordinator in L.A. and booked my place in his new training. I called the airlines and reserved my flights. I was ready to go. Actually, I couldn't wait to see him again. I would arrive on a Friday and the training was Saturday and Sunday. I was feeling excited and anxious at the same time. I wondered how I would feel when I actually saw him. I really didn't know anything about his private life at all now. *Was he single? Was he in love with someone new? If so, did I really want to know?* Yes, of course, I wanted to know. Almost three years had passed since we had been together. I had moved on. Well, that's what I kept telling myself anyway.

* * *

I arrived at the seminar early that morning, hoping to get a glimpse of Patrick before we started the day, but he was nowhere in sight. I waited impatiently inside the training room, wishing that we could have some way to connect beforehand. There were sixty people at this training. As I walked into the room, I noticed many massage tables set up all around the room with several chairs at each table. We were to find a table and sit down and wait for Patrick to arrive. My anxiety was now starting to escalate. How would I feel about him now? How would he feel about me? My heart raced and I was starting to feel overwhelmed about seeing him again after three years. I had thought I was over him and that I could be here without any worries, but all these old feelings for him starting rushing through my body. The room was spinning as if I were on a roller coaster ride. I could feel my stomach dropping. I realized that maybe I wasn't over him after all and that I had made a mistake by coming here.

Did I do the right thing?

As I approached the table to take my seat, there were two women and one man sitting in the chairs around the massage table. I sat down quickly. A petite, pretty blond woman about twenty years older than me began talking to me right away. She asked if I had done any of Patrick's seminars before or any private sessions with him.

"Yes," I replied. "How about you?"

She lit up as she told me she had known him for years, had taken many of his trainings and had numerous private sessions with him. The blonde and I hit it off instantly. Her name was Nancy and we became fast friends. I told her that I, too, knew Patrick for years and that he had made the biggest and most profound impact on my life than any other person ever.

She agreed and told me what a light in her life he had been. We both gushed for ten minutes about Patrick and his incredible work. I knew immediately Nancy and I were going to have lots to talk about during this weekend. All of a sudden the room chatter became very quiet. We all turned around to look as Patrick walked in from the back of the room.

Nancy and I were sitting right up front. He headed toward us as he walked slowly down the middle of the room. His piercing blue-green eyes stared straight into mine. My heart started to pound against my chest. He then smiled at me. For a moment I couldn't breathe, nor could I take my eyes off him either. He looked just as sexy and handsome as ever. I wondered what he was thinking about as he kept staring at me. I was still attracted to him but I noticed that it wasn't as intense as before. Maybe I was just protecting my heart or maybe I was picking up on something inside of him. Whatever it was, I felt a little relieved to be honest. I really wanted to focus on his teachings and not worry as much about him or what I was feeling toward him.

He started the day off the same way as all of his seminars—explaining about the ego and telling us about his experiences with body language, reading the unconscious signals and knowing how to remove negative thoughts from our body. At this point I wondered what new information he was going to be teaching here. I waited patiently as he continued teaching. After three hours of listening, there was still no new information yet. So when we had our first break I went up to him to ask if we were going to be learning any new things in this training. This was really bold, because in the past I would have never been able to confront him about his work or what he had planned. As I approached, he opened his arms wide and wrapped them tight around me. He still smelled delicious. "It's great to see you," he whispered.

"You too!" I didn't want to hug him very long. I couldn't handle too many of the feelings that were coming up. I asked him if we could talk for a moment. We stepped outside in the hallway by the door.

"I'm wondering what new information we are going to be learning. I came all the way from Dallas and I haven't heard anything new yet."

He looked stunned for a moment. He then took hold of my hand. "Stop worrying. We have a lot of time."

I could feel myself starting to become emotional. My eyes started to tear up a bit. Again he wrapped his nurturing arms around me and gave the sweetest hug ever. I wanted to just collapse in his arms right there and be swept off my feet. I hugged him tight and wanted so badly to kiss him. I wondered if he felt the same. I didn't even know if he was single or in a relationship. I just knew that my feelings for him were not all gone. In fact, they were starting to caress my body again like a cool summer breeze.

He whispered, "Can you give me a massage after the training? I really need some excellent work of yours."

Yes! Yes! I wanted to shout, but calmly said, "Of course I can." My mind started racing. *What does this mean? Does he want more? Or does he really just want a massage?* All I knew was that I had to play it cool or I would not be able to focus on the rest of his training.

As the day went on he broke us in to groups of two. My new friend Nancy and I had already decided that we would be partners for the day. We were to take turns holding one another's feet and feel intuitively what was going on in each other's body, thoughts, and feelings. This was different than before. Nancy and I had too much to share and talk about that we had a hard time listening to Patrick's directions. He kept giving us looks and you could plainly see that he was getting a little frustrated by our continuous chatting. At this point I had never met a complete stranger who I could talk to comfortably and share about the healing that Patrick did. It was such a relief to be able to connect with someone who really understood his work and what an incredible healer he was.

The rest of the day flew by and we were finally learning new things. He taught us how to go inside of ourselves and listen to our own intuition and to start trusting our feelings when we were working with someone. We learned that certain parts of the body held different emotions. He gave us a list of feelings and explained where these blocks would sometimes get stored in the many areas of our body. A block could potentially create a health issue if we didn't let go of these unresolved emotions. He reminded us that it is all connected through mind, body, and spirit. And that we are all connected, too. I was really understanding how much of my unhealed emotions were affecting not only my body but also my health, as well. As the training was finishing up, Patrick pulled me aside and said that he would be in his room in an hour.

"I have a table in the room. So no need to bring one." He gave me his room number. "I'll see you soon."

I just nodded. I was feeling apprehensive and uneasy. He was being very professional. A little too much. I wondered if I was going to see the fun, playful side of him or was it going to just be serious and work related with us now? After the seminar ended I had an hour to wait around before I would go to his room.

Nancy came up and said, "Hey, Donza, what are your plans for the evening?"

"I'm going to go work on Patrick in an hour."

She smiled. "Ah, you're so lucky! I wish I were going to work on him."

I knew that she really liked him too. Despite our budding friendship, I didn't tell her or anyone who lived in California about Patrick and me. Even though we weren't together anymore, I still felt like I needed to keep our business private.

Nancy and I stood outside the training room and chatted for most of the hour. I was grateful that I didn't wait alone for that time. I would have been driving myself crazy worrying over tonight's private session and wondering if anything more was going to be happening. Even though Patrick and I hadn't seen each other in years, I would still never be able to resist him. I must confess that there was a part of me that really wanted to rekindle the fire between us. I wasn't sure what was going to happen at this point.

The moment to find out had finally arrived and my heart surged. "Time to go meet Patrick." I took a deep breath and hugged Nancy. "See you tomorrow."

"Have fun." She smiled and walked away.

I headed for the elevator. The whole ride up I had butterflies swirling around my stomach. *Donza, you're about to be alone with him for the first time in three years . . .* My mind began racing. *Will I be swept off my feet again? Will there still be chemistry between us? God, what was I thinking agreeing to this?*

As I approached the door to his room, there was a quick moment of feeling as though maybe I had made a mistake by coming here. Not just to his room but to L.A. I wondered if he was feeling nervous too.

I knocked on the door and he opened it right away. I took a deep breath and before I could exhale, he took me in his arms and hugged me tight. I melted. I felt this warmth surging through my heart. Oh God, I still loved him. There was no denying it. I had grown a lot in the past three years. I wanted him to acknowledge it. I really needed that from him, especially since he was one of the reasons that my growth had accelerated. As intuitive as he was, I thought for sure that he could just look into my eyes and see that I was a totally transformed person, with more depth and abilities than ever before. The one he could now settle down with. So many thoughts flew by. *Is this really me thinking all of this? Where has all of my strength gone when it comes to Patrick? I thought I was all right. I'm over him. Aren't I?*

I had to get a grip, and fast. I pulled away from our hug. Yes, that felt good.

He immediately gave me a peck on my lips.

What is he joking? After three years of not seeing him and that's all I get!

I wanted to bombard him with questions and wanted him to ask about my life too.

Patrick said, "Thank you for coming up here to work on me."

"Sure." He had a massage table set up in the corner of his room. I walked over to it, doing my best to stay in a professional frame of mind. I sat against the table and asked nonchalantly, "So what's been going on with you?"

"I've just been working nonstop." He looked exhausted. "I haven't had any great bodywork since you last worked on me."

"Really?"

"I don't let many people work on my body. You know that."

I thought he was just being sweet, but it was true. He didn't allow anyone to touch him. He was too sensitive.

I sensed this gap between us, that we were both keeping our walls up. Before I started working on him, I felt we needed to talk and reconnect. "So, Patrick, what else is new?" What I really wanted to ask was: *Are you seeing someone? Are you in love?* I think there was a part of both of us that really didn't want to know, because he never asked anything about my personal life. He only asked how my business was going and if I was still body building. I felt that it was because he didn't want to tell me anything about *his* personal life. I felt very hurt that tonight he wasn't asking any questions at all about my life. Inside, a part of me wanted to break down and cry. I also knew that it would be much harder on me if we did reconnect on a romantic level again. To be honest, I was both solaced and disappointed that he was being so casual. We still had this very comfortable easy feeling with each other. It was now just different.

We stared at one another for a long, dangerous moment. I turned around and focused on prepping the massage table. I hadn't brought any oil or cream and was hoping that he had some. Doing a massage without oils was like trying to paint without a brush . . . just wasn't going to happen.

"Do you have any cream I can use to work on you?" I asked.

"Yes, I have some lotion."

I leaned against the table and crossed my arms. "Before I get started I have a question for you . . . Do you remember the very first time I worked on you and you had those tiny silver sparkles fly out of your nose? What were they?"

He grinned like a mischievous little boy and shrugged his shoulders.

"Oh, my God, are you serious? You're still not going to tell me what they were? Come on, Patrick, you gotta tell me something."

Again he just looked at me and smiled, without a hint of letting me know. This was like a game to him. I didn't like it because it made me feel as though he was hiding something. Or maybe that he was always going to be playing the teacher role in my life. Even after years of constant work and growth I had done on myself, I felt that I was never going to be enough or that I would never be an equal to him. I felt that we were only going to be friends from this point on. No matter what I was feeling I had to let go of all of my dreams and fantasies that I had for him. I had to hide everything I was feeling, because he would pick up on it and I didn't want to become emotional in front of him. Especially when I was going to be working on him now. I decided to stay in my professional work mode and only speak about business and treat him like any other client.

I told him to get on the table and that I was going to be very quiet so he could just relax. I didn't want to read his body at all. I just wanted to get through this session without breaking down or him asking any questions about how I was feeling. I literally switched off my feelings. I had never done that before. I knew I had to if I was going to be able to do the massage. I'm sure he knew what I was doing because he, too, became very quiet and didn't say another word during the session. I felt relieved and sad at the same time, because I only had one more day with him in the training. Whatever I was feeling about him I kept to myself and just focused on my work.

After the session, he raved about how much he enjoyed my work and how he never lets anyone work on him.

"So you feel better then?" I asked.

"Yes, much better. You are the best! Thank you." He walked towards me with his arms outstretched. It was like there was this magnetic force field pulling us together. There was no way I could resist him. I welcomed him with open arms. And my heart sank to my stomach.

"I've missed you," he whispered softly in my ear.

I could feel myself starting to melt again. Before I could stop myself I whispered, "I've missed you too."

He kissed my lips gently and then pulled away. I wanted to pull him back and kiss him without abandon, to fall together into the overwhelming feelings of sexual intensity. To feel his lips kissing mine so passionately. Exploring my body. He was the best kisser and I missed getting lost in our kissing.

I couldn't succumb to my desires though. As much as I wanted to I just stopped. I felt at this moment that there would never be anyone who could ever take his place and that there was a connection with him that was never going to be broken. We shared something deep on a sacred soul level that there was no way for us to ever be disconnected. Even if we weren't together romantically or as a couple, I felt that Patrick was always going to a part of me. This knowingness felt expansive and a sense of freedom filled my body with peace and clarity.

Chapter Twenty-six

$\times$ $\cdot$ $\cdot$ $\times$ $\times$ $\cdot$ $\times$
$\cdot$ $\times$ $\cdot$ $\cdot$

As I walked into the training room the next day, my mind kept thinking back to the night before. How Patrick had kept it light and professional. How we still had a connection but there wasn't anything romantic happening between us. I felt sad and a little confused by his behavior and my mixed emotions. Today was the last day with him and I didn't have a clue when I would see him again.

Nancy spotted me right away. "Hi, Donza!" She rushed over and greeted me with a friendly hug. "So how did it go last night?"

"It was great." I tried to sound as cool and casual. I knew that she was going to want to know more details. I could never tell her all the things that were stirring deep inside me.

"What was it like to work on him?" Nancy asked.

I shrugged. "I've worked on him before." I didn't want to answer a lot of questions so I immediately asked, "How are you doing?"

Before she could answer, Patrick walked in and the room became very quiet. *Thank God.* I whispered, "Nancy, let's talk later on the break."

The seminar cruised by fast that morning. We did more practicing on each other's bodies. Patrick came around to each table and watched us all working with one another. He wanted to hear what we were feeling and picking up on from different parts of the body. I didn't feel nervous at all like usual. I'm guessing that was because I knew what I was doing more and felt comfortable with what we were learning. What was really great about this day was that we were able to be on the table and receive over an hour of intuitive, profound healing and bodywork from different people in our group. Also, having Patrick there watching and giving us feedback on how we were doing was one of the best parts of the training. He was able to spend more time with each person and you could really feel how present he was with everyone. That was such a gift to us all because he made you feel like you were the only one he was talking to. Patrick's complete presence was one of the many things I fell in love with him for and really missed.

At our first break Nancy came over right away to talk. I knew that she wanted to know more about my time with Patrick. I had to be careful and not say too much. For she, too, was intuitive and had taken all of Patrick's trainings and did many private sessions with him. I would never tell her about our private life together. I kept it brief and just told her it went great.

"Are you going to see him later after the seminar?" she asked.

"I don't know." He hadn't said anything so I wasn't planning on it, although I would if he needed to see me.

The rest of the day went by even faster than the morning session. I was starting to feel very sad not knowing when or if I would see Patrick again. I decided that at the end of the day I would ask him if he had any plans to come back to Dallas to do anymore trainings. I wanted to see if he was interested in seeing me again while he was there. I felt that I was more mature and could handle myself better now, even though I knew it would be risky thinking about opening up emotionally with him again. I also hadn't met anyone that I was remotely interested in, nor had I ever felt a closeness and depth the way I felt with him. Part of me wanted to risk it all. While the other part knew how long it took me to heal from the last time he broke things off.

As the training was coming to a close, I sat there waiting anxiously while we all applauded and thanked him for such an incredible training. For me, the weekend was a success. I was happy that I came and reconnected with him.

After the seminar, several people wanted his attention and time. It was always hard to get him out because everyone wanted to talk with him. As I approached the long line of people, he looked my way a few times with a slight hint of a smile and that longer look that only we would know about. It still made me feel all warm inside. Finally it was my turn to thank him and say good-bye. Without saying a word he took me in his arms. We stood there hugging and I could still feel so much love and connection with him. I knew he felt it too. As I pulled away first, I thanked him for an amazing weekend.

"So do you have any plans to come back to Dallas anytime soon?" I asked.

"No, I don't."

My heart sank a little.

As I started to say good-bye he grabbed hold of my hand. He then leaned in to kiss me on the cheek. "You keep in touch, you hear?" He winked. After all this time he could still make my knees go weak with just one single wink. I winked back and then gave him the biggest smile ever.

"I love you," he whispered.

"I love you too."

The time had come to really say good-bye and mean it. I had allowed the fantasy to continue on way too long, wishing on some level that he would always want to be with me and that somehow we would get back together. It was time to let go completely and move forward with my life knowing that he would not be in it in the same way anymore. It all felt bitter sweet.

As I left the seminar, I kept thinking about one of his first trainings I took and how he had told us that we wanted things that were familiar, because that would make us feel safe. Patrick was truly right about that. He did feel safe and familiar. I understood this process in a new way now. I was ready to let him go.

I finally did.

PART FOUR
Bliss

Chapter Twenty-seven

Over the next fifteen years, my life went on a fast track of spiritual and emotional growth. I traveled all over the world taking many different healing seminars, self-help programs, and did extensive amounts of therapy. I studied different religions, philosophies, and healing methods. The workshops I took helped me evolve and grow more than I ever thought possible. Doing inner work on myself became one of my greatest passions. I focused on my life, career, and healing, and from this inward journey I discovered my true purpose. I knew that I was here to help people open up to their fullest potential. If I could do it, then so could they.

Nancy and I became very close friends over the years. Through her I learned that Patrick had met someone and that he was getting married. I can honestly say I was happy for him. I never told Nancy anything about us. She still lived in Los Angeles and was seeing him for private healing sessions. Although I was very curious and wanted to know who Patrick's fiancé was and what kind of women he fell in love with, I knew that he was part of my past now and that it wasn't any of my business. I only had gratitude and prayed that one day I would meet someone who could fill my heart and stimulate my mind and spirit the same way that Patrick could. Someone who was spiritually aware, emotionally sensitive, passionate about their work, and ready to go deeper within themselves. I was ready for an equal relationship now. The bar was set extremely high. I wondered if it were possible to ever find what I was yearning for since I knew what I was looking for and his shoes were some big ones to fill.

As the years passed I began creating success in my life on many levels. I started my own massage business, specializing in sports massage, and I became a life coach. My world took off in a way that I never imagined possible. I worked on famous athletes, actors, rock stars, authors, and many affluent people all over the world. I was no longer this shy, self conscious, immature woman anymore. All of the work made such an invaluable difference and paid off in my life. The only thing that was missing was love. There was still this little part in the back of my mind that would always compare all of my relationships to Patrick. At first, I wasn't consciously aware that I was doing it. But after three different men in my life asked me to marry them and each time I found a reason why I couldn't—even when I loved them—I knew that I had to keep doing work on myself to find the answers within.

Chapter Twenty-eight

When the spring of 2008 arrived, I received a call from my dear friend, Megan, who lives in Providence, Rhode Island. She told me that there was a man coming to town who did the same kind of work that Patrick did. I was intrigued. This man was actually trained by Patrick and said that he was still in contact with him. I casually asked her to please give him my email address to give to Patrick. Within days I received a brief email from Patrick. I was stunned. We hadn't communicated for so long!

In the email, he asked if I was married and had children. He wanted to know how I was doing and if I still lived in Dallas. I emailed him back immediately, answering all his questions. I told him I was single and still lived in Dallas. I then asked him all of the same questions. I didn't hear back from him for weeks. When he finally emailed me back, I learned that he was single and still living in Los Angeles, doing his work and much more. At that time in my life one of my closest friends, Vaal, who I had known for twenty-five years, was dying of cancer and I let him know that. My friend passed away in September that year and I never heard anything again from Patrick at that point. I was disappointed, I must confess.

Months passed. Then February of 2009 I received a friend request on Facebook from Patrick along with a message: *I'm sorry for being so quiet. I have now stopped to smell the roses. You look amazing.*

Suddenly our passionate romance started to be rekindled. He called every day and we exchanged seventy-two emails within three weeks. All my feelings for him resurfaced. After not seeing one another for fifteen years, the excitement, intensity, and curiosity were building up inside of both of us. I was no longer a young, inexperienced, naïve woman. I had matured and evolved in so many ways that I wondered if he would even know or understand who I had become. We didn't know each other at all anymore. We were completely starting over. The thought of seeing him again was overwhelming and thrilling at the same time. By the time that we decided on a date to see each other, our relationship was back on full force. We were more excited to see each other than ever. The attention, compliments, and openness we shared were so beautiful. I didn't think it was possible to reconnect this deeply again. The intensity between us that was present was much stronger than before. The love that flourished opened our hearts once more. I could now take him in on a whole deeper level.

When our plans to meet in L.A. in March of 2009 were confirmed, my excitement couldn't be contained. I was going to be spending four days with him. He even took off work for those four days, which for Patrick was a really big deal. This was the most time that we would be spending with each other. I was feeling very anxious along with joy and sheer enthusiasm.

Chapter Twenty-nine

This brings us back to where my story began. I had flown to L.A. and met Patrick in at his high-rise apartment building in Beverly Hills. Even after fifteen years he still looked gorgeous and could melt my heart with his gaze. We had kissed briefly in the lobby. He had teased me, telling me I was in big trouble. I asked him to kiss me some more. Instead he invited to take me to lunch.

As we arrived at the sushi restaurant, we couldn't keep our hands off each other as he sat next to me in the booth. I loved that he didn't sit across from me. No man had ever done that before. He wanted to be close and started rubbing my leg and stroking my hands. I couldn't stop touching him either. I wished that we would have just skipped lunch and gone straight up to his apartment. He was all the food I needed. The anticipation and waiting that was building up between us was almost more than I could handle. I couldn't wait to be naked in his arms again and feel our passion together once more.

By the time we arrived back to his apartment building, I was shaking inside. How we were able to control ourselves the entire elevator ride up was beyond me. We walked into his place, closed the door, then without any hesitation he grabbed me with such intensity. It was on! He started kissing me with more passion than I had ever felt from him before. We both trembled with such excitement and desire. So many extraordinary feelings flooded my entire body, mind, and spirit. There was something happening between us that had never occurred before. This feeling of pure energy and passion ignited us in a whole new way. Years and years of unexpressed feelings emerged. I had all this ecstatic energy pulsating throughout my body. Together we explored each other's depth, where all of our feelings were being unleashed in this dynamic, profound moment. We couldn't get enough of one another. I was able to take in all of his passion, love, sensuality, and completely allow it to consume every fiber of my being. There was a spiritual connection and sexual energy that was so present and powerful that I felt intense emotions. Tears rolled down my face as he just kept loving me and being in tune with every feeling I was having. I felt safe and connected with him. Memories from all the times I was with him coursed through me, as if no time had passed between us. We just picked up from where we had left off fifteen years earlier. All I could think about was that I would get four fabulous days with him, and it was starting out more perfectly than I could have ever imagined.

We spent the whole afternoon making love and getting to know each other more deeply than ever before. I was falling in love all over again, and my heart opened wider than ever. This time I knew I would never have to look any further. I had the man of my dreams and he was everything I had been looking and waiting for, for so long. The joy and happiness I felt with him was consuming. I knew he was feeling it too. He kept smiling and making these sweet little sounds of pleasure as we stayed snuggled up in his big, beautiful bed. As he got up to go to the bathroom, I remembered a mystery about him that always had me curious. I climbed out of the bed and walked toward the bathroom. As he came out, I stood in front of him with my arms stretched wide open to hug him.

"I have a question for you," I whispered in his ear. "What were those tiny silver sparkles that came out of your nose years ago when I first worked on you? Can you please tell me now?"

"Wow, Donza, you are the most persistent woman I have ever met."

"Yes, and I'm going to keep asking until you finally tell me."

Patrick smiled. "What you witnessed was proof that there's more to this world than meets the eye. Those sparkles were pure energy made up of negative thought forms and emotions. Like an alchemist, you moved and released that dark energy from my body and transformed them into particles of loving light. Not many healers can do that. Plus you saw them. Just like I witnessed miracles back in India. I knew that you weren't ready to understand it then and I didn't want to freak you out. You were so young and innocent. I never had anyone work on my body that was as clear as you were. That's why I knew you were special."

"Really, are you serious? You mean for twenty two-years I've wondered about what that was coming out of your nose, and it was healing energy? I have never to this day seen that happen with anyone else."

"You never worked on anyone like me before." He grinned.

"Yes, that is for sure."

Then he pulled me into his arms and we kissed again and again, barely coming up for air.

I love him! I love him! I kept thinking in my head.

He stopped kissing me abruptly and looked in my eyes. "I love you. I love you."

As I heard his voice echoing my thoughts, I felt as though I was going to faint.

"I love you too!" I said with the biggest smile.

* * *

It was now evening and we were both hungry. We ordered Thai food and talked more over dinner. Afterward, Patrick drew the most luscious bath for us. I never had a man do that before. He was all about my needs. He bought all of my favorite foods, water, and wine. He had thought of everything before I arrived and had it all waiting for me. *I could get really used to this*, I thought.

I showered him with compliments with every small deed that he did. I wasn't used to being taken care of like this. I had always imagined what it would feel like to have my partner be as thoughtful and caring as I was. Patrick surpassed all of my expectations by far. Yes, I was falling in love with him again and I was willing to risk it all. This time he was too. His way of showing love was through the love channel I so desperately needed. He was very affectionate, did such great acts of kindness and services for me. Plus he was so giving with everything. What I valued most was the time Patrick took off work to spend with me.

We had fifteen years to catch up on. We sat on his patio for hours and I was in heaven listening to all the fascinating stories about his life. He loved talking and sharing the things he taught and the work he was doing. He also liked to smoke outside, which I still couldn't stand. He smoked more than anyone I had ever known. Never before would I ever think of dating a smoker, let alone fall back in love with one. But for Patrick I was willing to tolerate it. I was trying really hard not to judge him or complain too much about his smoking. The truth was I really wanted him to stop. Vibrant health was a big value on my list of what I wanted in a man. This was the only issue I had with him.

That first night as we were lying in bed, he revealed that he was going to have a minor procedure done on his heart in two weeks. I started to worry. I couldn't believe that he waited to tell me this. Of course he didn't want me to worry or be concerned. He reassured me that it was no big deal and that he would be fine.

Several years before he had many issues with his heart because of a heart defect. Now they were going to go in through his leg and repair some arteries—a simple procedure that he had done before. He didn't seem worried at all. As a matter of fact, he really didn't have any concern or much emotion about it. That bothered me because I felt that he was being way to cool about it, not telling the whole story. He had too much pride and would never let anyone see him ill or under the weather. He would never allow anyone to help him. He would hire someone if he needed it.

I asked him many questions about this "procedure." Come to find out it was a serious operation and that he would be under for hours. I freaked out. I felt this sick feeling inside my stomach. Anxiety began to take over my body like an infectious disease. He knew right away that I was having a "moment." He wrapped his arms around me and enveloped me in his warm, nurturing energy, holding me tight.

"I'm going to be all right, Donza. Really, I will be fine."

"Why are you still smoking if you have heart problems? This makes no sense at all. We just found each other again and now you're about to go through something so dangerous." I could feel the tears coming. I didn't want to cry but I couldn't hold them in any longer. I had just lost my best friend six months earlier from cancer. She, too, used to smoke, and my mother died because she wouldn't stop smoking. "I'm so scared," I whimpered. "If anything happens to you I don't know what I would do."

"I'm going to be just fine." He sighed and kissed my cheek over and over, trying to ease my fears.

I started in with more questions. "How long is the surgery? How long will you be in the hospital? How long will it take for you to recover?"

"Will you relax? I am going to tell you everything."

There was no way I could relax. After he shared all of the

details, I asked him again if I could be there at the hospital for him. One of his best guy friends was going to be there to help if he needed it. He said, "no, thank you," to my offer and that his friend would call me or I could call his friend to check up on him anytime. He would be in the hospital for at least a week. The recovery time was six to eight weeks. I wouldn't be seeing him while he has healing. I never met a man who didn't want anyone there to take care of him. Patrick was very private and he didn't want anyone he cared about to worry or stress over him during his time of recovery. He had such calmness about it when he talked, and his attitude was positive. He acted as if it were no big deal. I wish I could say that he was able to ease my fears and worries with his casual demeanor, but he didn't.

There was nothing I could do to help if he really didn't want it. I just listened and kept more quiet than usual. He knew I was processing all this upsetting information. I could feel myself wanting to put the brakes on my feelings toward him. I wanted to be there for him, and I was really sad that he was choosing to go through all of this alone. If I would have known about his surgery earlier I would have stayed longer. I loved him deeply and knew I wouldn't be able to stop my feelings for him, even If I wanted to. I also respected his wishes, so I reassured him that I would be there if he did change his mind.

I now knew that I had to step it up in these next four days and make sure that we had more fun, passion, intimacy, and excitement than ever before. I was going to show how much I loved and appreciated him in every way I could imagine. Get to know him better and make this precious time of ours together count. He was thinking about it, too, because he went out of his way to express his love and affection, hoping that I would notice.

I did notice everything and appreciated every romantic gesture.

Chapter Thirty

Each day Patrick and I spent together was absolutely magical. We worked on each other every day. He had a massage table set up in his office. I would give him massages and he would read my body, remove blocks, and adjust my neck. He did the most amazing thing to my ears. He was able to adjust my ears and open up my hearing more. He said that it also helped with listening and taking in information easier. I told him that I was getting migraines. He said he could take them away. I believed every word he spoke, especially when it came to his healing abilities. I trusted him completely and he trusted me. I was always learning and growing so much in his presence. He had a unique gift in the way he shared information. He was the most knowledgeable man on every subject. He could discuss just about anything. Being with him, I felt smarter than before. Still after all these years, he was present in every moment we shared together. He had such a peaceful effect on me and at the same time could ignite this passion deep in my soul like no other.

As long as I was entering into this new relationship with him, I had to allow myself to be as open and vulnerable with my feelings as I possibly could. These four days did just that. I now had the opportunity to spend time with him, expressing every thought and feeling. We both wanted to know about the last fifteen years of each other's lives.

On our second day together, he took me shopping on Rodeo Drive again in Beverly Hills. I remembered when he first took me there twenty-two years earlier. I was young and I had never seen anything like it before.

As Patrick was driving and looking for a parking space, I said, "Do you know that I still have the piece of jade you gave me all those years ago? I've kept it with me for protection just like you said." I pulled it out of my purse to show him.

"Donza, I can't believe you kept it all these years. This means so much to me." He parked the car and leaned over and kissed me. It was special moments like this that made the most impact on us. He understood the profound difference that he had made in my life. He appreciated how much I listened and always cherished our times we had shared and the many gifts we gave to each other.

We were both happy as we held hands and strolled the streets of Beverly Hills. He wanted to shop for cologne. Also, he wanted to buy me anything that I wanted. *I have everything I need right here*, I thought, squeezing his hand. I had a fun time shopping with him, and I let him know that I didn't need anything. I felt comfortable now with myself and knew that I was no longer out of my depth. I could finally afford to shop on Rodeo Drive if I chose to. I watched him buy his favorite Armani cologne and enjoyed seeing him happy. I wanted to only focus on the moment because so many times I felt myself starting to get worried about his surgery. He always knew when I was thinking about it and told me to stop. Was he really not concerned or was he just playing Mr. Cool so not to alarm me? Each time I felt my thoughts drifting on anything that wasn't in the moment I just stopped and refocused on the present.

After hours of shopping, it was time to go back to his apartment and have some more *real* fun. There was never a moment when I didn't feel passion or desire for him. I felt closer and closer each time we were intimate. The spiritual connection was deepening as we gazed into each other's eyes, breathing and holding eye contact. Our long history and love strengthened our bond. It was as if two souls had finally reunited and were once again merging together as one. The familiar feelings we shared reached a new level of depth, maybe because we both had grown over the years. He was my soul mate and there wasn't anything I could do now to stop my heart from opening up more and more with every minute we were together. We had many things to offer one another in this relationship. I was the one he put on the pedestal now. Finally, I felt that I was enough and that I deserved to be with such a beautiful, spiritual man. All the work I had done on myself paid off. I was with the man of my dreams. Even though I had many fears about his upcoming surgery and the six to eight weeks that I would have to be away from him during his healing process, I knew that we had a profound purpose for coming back together at this time in our lives.

Chapter Thirty-one

Each morning we woke up and sat outside on the patio. He smoked and drank his French coffee. He would grind the beans fresh every day. I wasn't a coffee drinker, although he wanted me to be. We would snuggle close together and start the morning with plenty of affection. This was the time when we really were able to get to know each other even more. He loved to talk as much as I did. That was a very rare thing to find a man who could keep up with my chatterbox self. I never once was bored listening to him. It was always a constant flow in conversation. Patrick loved listening to all of my stories and adventures too. I loved this precious time we had each morning. It started our day out perfectly. There was nowhere we needed to be, except with each other in those moments. I was starting to picture my life with him again. This time we were both finally ready.

As my final two days with him dashed by, I began to feel sad and anxious. He showed more love to me than I had ever felt in my life from anyone before. On the third evening, he even cooked the most delicious meal—fresh scallops, creamy mashed potatoes, and asparagus with a sweet glaze sauce. I wasn't allowed to help him at all. I sat at the counter and watched him cook as he played his music in the background. Enigma was what he chose to listen to. I never saw anyone look as happy and pleased with himself as he cooked. This was another one of my love channels, cooking for me. It was such a turn on.

Before he set the table, he asked me to go wait out on the patio until everything was ready.

What is he up to? I wondered. Within a few minutes he was ready. I walked in and couldn't believe my eyes. There were two candles lit in the middle of the table and a lovely table cloth. The table was set with gorgeous black dishes with white trim and cloth napkins on the side of each plate. It looked like I had just stepped into a four-star restaurant. As he pulled the chair out, I looked down to see a little gift-wrapped box sitting on the chair. I glanced up at him with a surprise on my face.

He smiled. "Open it."

I put my hand to my chest. "What did you do? What is it?"

"Something special I found for you. Just open it."

I tore open the package as if I were a child opening a gift on Christmas morning. I was hoping to see an attractive piece of jewelry or something that I might be able to wear on my finger. I lifted the lid off the box and there was this sparkling, beautiful, blue citrine stone. It had these crystal clusters around the bottom of the stone and the most unusual shape I had ever seen. It was about one and a half inches tall and wide. I gently lifted the stone out of the box to take a closer look. I was a little confused, I must confess. It was really a gorgeous stone, but it wasn't jewelry or like any kind of a gift I had ever received from a man before. Although, he did give me the piece of jade years before. That was very precious to me. When the puzzled look swept across my face, I was sure that he noticed.

"What is it?" I said as I tried not to crinkle my nose.

"This is a powerful stone I brought back when I was in India.

It has been blessed by many gurus and is said to have medicinal energy, especially if you hold it when you meditate. Also, I have put my own healing energy and love into it myself for you."

I covered my mouth with my hand and once again felt the tears starting to well up. I reached across the table and threw my arms around him. I stood there squeezing him and kissing his neck. I knew that this gift meant the world to him.

"Thank you! I love it! Most of all I love what it means and that you put your love and energy into it. I love you so much!" By this time I was crying.

"I love you, too," he whispered as he kept kissing my cheeks ever so softly.

We sat down and I enjoyed the best dinner that anyone had ever cooked for me. Everything smelled and tasted delicious. I showered him with compliments and let him know how much I appreciated all of his work. To him it was fun and no work at all.

After dinner we went for a walk along the beach. The sand through my toes and smelling the fresh ocean air were just what I needed to forget that we only had one more night together. I knew I couldn't even think about leaving tomorrow or the water works would start all over again. We walked side by side with our arms wrapped around each other's back. His fingers kept gently stroking and gliding down my back. I loved those soft, tender strokes. My body melted with each loving touch. One of the things I noticed the most about Patrick now was that he was much more playful than before. He was really funny and knew how to tell a joke with such perfect timing. I was also very playful and loved jokes. I also liked to wrestle. I had practiced a few different Martial Arts over the years for fun. So when he kept teasing and trying to tickle me, I told him I was going to tackle him down on the sand and wrestle him until he surrendered. He started laughing and wanted to see just how tough I was. Little did I know, Patrick was trained and knew a lot more self-defense than I did. I tried to wrestle him, but he took off down the beach.

"I used to be tough but not anymore!" I yelled. "But I'm freakishly strong though." I ran as fast as I could to catch him. I grabbed hold of his shirt and down he went. As I fell on top of him, we started rolling around in the sand. Within seconds we were kissing and barely coming up for air. We couldn't stop laughing and kissing. It's moments like this that will forever be imprinted in my memories.

* * *

Our final night together in L.A. was much more than I could have ever expected. I saw many different, wonderful sides to him—the romantic, the caregiver, and his great sense of humor, which kept us laughing throughout my visit. I felt his heart open up as he shared himself deeply and honestly. Most of all, I felt his spiritual connection that was strong and inspiring. His unconditional love, nurturing, and compassion brought new hope not only in my life, but in my heart. In these four days with him I found a little piece of myself hidden deep within that I had never discovered before. I, too, could love unconditionally, even through all of my many fears and constant worries. Patrick helped make that possible through his constant loving presence. I couldn't wait to share the rest of my life with my extraordinary soul mate.

We stayed up for hours kissing and talking on the couch with my head nestled in his lap. Later he picked me up and carried me to the bedroom. We spent a whole night together where I didn't know where he started or where I began. It was wonderful to feel this closeness with him, a feeling that would stay with me forever.

* * *

When I woke up the next morning, he was cuddled up so close to my body that I couldn't move. I loved it! I nerve-stroked his face lightly with my fingers as he started waking up. This was the last morning with him for a while. I wanted it to be the most memorable time that we shared. I rolled on top of him and kissed him from head to toe. My sensual, goddess self had emerged and taken over. He surrendered quickly. I made love to that man in a way I had never done before. We would never be forgetting this morning together, not ever. After making love, we lay in each other's arms.

Soon I had to face the fact that I was leaving and didn't know how long it would be until we saw each other again. This road felt way too familiar. I didn't want to put myself through it again, although it was different this time. We were committed and in love. I was successful enough now that I could move for him. We just had to get through his surgery and have him back on his feet. That was the main focus now, seeing him healthy and well.

We sat out on the patio and were very quiet at first. I only had a few hours left before I had to go to the airport. I had my rental car so he wasn't taking me there. It was going to be very difficult to leave him, especially since we didn't know how long his recovery would be. The surgery was going to be on March 16, just seven days away.

I began to ask more of what he was feeling about it all. Again, he reassured me that it wasn't a big deal and that he would be just fine. It was more of an inconvenience to him because he had to take time off of work. He would still work twelve to fourteen hours a day, never slowing down. He loved his work but his body was telling him it was time to take it easy now.

"Are you going to finally stop smoking after this surgery?"

"Yes, that's my plan."

I was happy to hear that. I wanted to believe it, but it is one of the hardest habits to break. "Are you sure that you don't need me to be here for you? I really want do anything I can to help."

"Thank you. I promise I would tell you if I thought I needed help."

Since he wouldn't accept my help I let it go and trusted that he would be okay. I didn't want to spend our last few hours together upset or worrying. We stayed outside, curled up in each other's arms, talking and planning for my next visit. I was really going to miss all of the touch and contact I had with him. Along with everything else that was important. This is when I realized that quality time was the most important thing to me in a relationship, just being able to be. Not doing anything, just being. I was never like that before. As a matter of fact, I had to always be doing something. Just living in the moment was a nice change of pace and another wonderful gift Patrick gave to my life.

It was now close to lunch time and he had another surprise for me. He made us lunch while I was getting showered, packed, and ready to leave. He always wanted to nurture and take care of my needs. Within thirty minutes he had everything ready and waiting. He started out with a scrumptious fruit salad with all of my favorite fruits: mangos, blueberries, pineapples, strawberries, with this poppy seed dressing. It was delicious. He made fresh salmon with lemon and steamed veggies over a bed of brown rice. I was speechless. How he whipped this up so quickly was unbelievable. I kept hugging, kissing, and thanking him for his incredible thoughtfulness. Before I could finish my words, he walked us over to his closet by the front door. As he opened it, hanging alone in the closest was this gorgeous, black leather jacket.

"Try it on to see if it fits," he said with such pride. "I thought this looked like you."

I slipped the jacket on. "I love it! It's totally my style! Thank you, but you didn't have to get me anything else. You've done so much already."

"Nonsense. It looks great on you," he said. "I love seeing you smile."

I leaned in to give him a light peck, thinking that we were going to be eating lunch. It must have finally hit him that I was leaving, because all of a sudden he was passionately kissing me like I was the only thing that mattered in the world. Lunch waited. It was the perfect ending to my trip.

* * *

After lunch it was time to for me leave. Patrick went into his bathroom as I gathered the rest of my things. He came out holding his cologne bottle—Halston Z-14. He put some on and then handed me the bottle. "I know you love this, so you take the rest home with you and think of me."

"Really, I can have it?" I thought it was a little odd that he gave away his favorite cologne, but I thanked him for it.

He said, "I'll get some more later."

We took the elevators down to his underground parking, never once letting go of one another. He loaded the car and walked around to the driver's side to open my door. I told him that I wasn't going to cry and that I would call him as soon as I landed back in Dallas. We held on tight to each other. His cologne intoxicated me. We kissed, not wanting our time together to end. We must have stood there for twenty minutes or more. I could feel many intense emotions bubbling up to the surface. I knew I had to get out of there quickly or I would completely lose it.

"I love you," he said. "You are very special to me, do you know that?"

I nodded. "I love you so much. Thank you for showing all your love to me. Yes, you are one extraordinary man." I reached into my purse and handed him a card that I had written. I told him not to read it until I was on the plane. It was one of those mushy, romantic love notes that thanked him for an incredible four days.

He leaned in the open window to kiss my lips one final time. "I love you," he whispered.

I felt tears coming up. I said it back to him quickly and then drove out of there as fast as I could. I put my sunglasses on and allowed my tears to fall. I cried all the way to LAX. I had so many feelings going on inside that I wasn't sure how I would be able to function. *I should be happy,* I thought. *I'm in love. Then why all of these intense emotions?* I was worried about his surgery and all. Yet this felt different. I had to get a grip on myself. I wasn't sure what was going on. I just wanted the crying to stop.

PART FIVE

Turbulence

Chapter Thirty-two

I arrived back in Dallas very late that night emotionally exhausted. I called Patrick to let him know I made it back. We had a brief conversation and I told him we would talk later when I wasn't so tired.

In the morning I woke up to the sweetest email from him, saying how much he missed my body next to his and that he really enjoyed our time together. Also that he was going to be very busy before the surgery. He told me he loved me and that we would talk later. It was short and sweet.

I wrote him back saying how much I missed him already and that I couldn't wait to have all of this behind us. I wanted to be supportive and positive for him. I reassured him that I was here if he needed anything at all. Later that day I received a text from him: *Thinking about you and missing you. XO*

I loved hearing from him, especially knowing how busy he was. I wondered how he was really coping with it all privately. Each time we spoke that week he seemed to be positive and upbeat. He still didn't seem worried about the surgery. I didn't say much about it until the night before he was to go to the hospital. He made sure

I had his best friend's number so I could check on him. I started getting emotional and couldn't control my tears. I didn't want to upset him but I was scared for him, and for myself. I didn't know what I would do if something happened to him.

"I'm going to get through this just fine. Do you trust me, Donza?"

"Yes, of course I do. I'm just worried and wish I were there for you."

"You *are* here for me. So stop worrying."

"I'm sorry I'm being like this," I whimpered. "This is about you. I must stop this now."

"I won't be able to talk for a while, so make sure you call my friend."

"I will call him all the time. I hope he doesn't get tired of me." I felt a lot better after our conversation. We took a long time to say our good-byes that night. We must have said "I love you" ten times before we finally hung up. His surgery was out of my hands. The only thing I could do was pray, which I did for most of that night.

* * *

That morning I kept watching the clock, waiting till the moment I knew he would be going in. I called many of my friends for prayer support. The surgery was supposed to be three hours long. I could call his friend anytime after that. Patrick had introduced us on the phone when I was in L.A. It was early afternoon when I made my first call. I was relieved when Patrick's friend answered right away.

"Hi, this is Donza. How's he doing?"

"Well, he's still in surgery."

"Is everything okay?"

"As far as I know everything's fine."

I asked how Patrick was feeling before he went in. His friend assured me that he had been in high spirits and feeling great. I was relieved to hear that. I knew Patrick well enough to know he would never let anyone know if he were nervous or scared.

"I thought the surgery would be done by now," I said. "How much longer do you think?"

"I'm not sure. Can I call you as soon as I hear something?"

"Yes, or I'll check back in a little while. Thank you so much," I said, feeling grateful. If it weren't for him I'm not sure what I would have done to get information. It would have been much harder on me for sure.

Time crept by that afternoon. I was filled with anxiety and worry that I didn't know what to do with myself. Three more hours went by and still no word. Finally, I called his friend back. Patrick was just getting out of surgery. It took almost six hours. He made it through but there were some complications. They severed a nerve in his right leg and it was going to take longer to heal than expected. The doctors were going to keep him knocked out for a few days to help with the pain. They didn't want any extra stress on his heart.

I never felt so relieved in my life. He still wasn't completely out of danger but the great news was that he survived the surgery. This became my life for the next few weeks. I talked to his friend every day, sometimes twice a day to check on his progress. Patrick was in a lot of pain and wasn't eating at all. He was very weak and had no energy whatsoever. He couldn't talk nor did he want to. The doctors kept him in the hospital for nine days. I never once spoke to him during that time. I prayed for him constantly. I hated that I couldn't be there with him in his time of illness. All I cared about was his healing and him feeling well enough to speak and eat. He had lost thirty pounds. He was a small, thin-framed guy to begin with. He didn't have it to lose.

I couldn't wait to hear his voice again. I called his phone just to hear his voice. It went straight to voicemail. I left him many messages so that he would know that I had been thinking of him every day.

Finally after two weeks I received a text from Patrick: *I'm still alive. Hope you are well. Love you.*

I jumped up and down with joy! I texted him back: *I love you and see you healing more every day. You rest all you can. I'm here if you need me.*

He didn't respond and I was okay with that. I still called his friend every few days to check on him. He kindly filled me in about everything that was going on with Patrick's health. He was suffering so much with his leg and still couldn't walk. He didn't feel like talking on the phone. They had him on so much pain medication and antibiotics that he was weak as a kitten.

Four weeks went by and I still hadn't heard from him, although his friend and I were getting to know each other well by now. Patrick couldn't talk yet. I began to get very worried. I needed contact, if not physical then at least a text or a call. I had thought he was healing more, so why didn't he want to talk? When I confronted his friend, he assured me that it wasn't me, that Patrick felt exhausted all the time and that the drugs were taking their toll on his body and affecting his moods. I then knew that this was way more serious than he had let on about. He was sicker and his heart was in worse shape than maybe he even knew.

Chapter Thirty-three

The end of April came and it had been almost six weeks that I hadn't talked to him. I didn't know what to think or feel. I tried to be as patient and understanding as possible but I felt that something was terribly wrong. That perhaps it wasn't just his illness that was keeping him from calling. I felt so confused and went over everything in my head a thousand times to make sure I didn't miss anything. We had departed on such loving terms. So what was the issue? Why hadn't he called or texted? What had changed?

I called his friend one final time and told him to please have Patrick call me. I was almost in tears by this time. I asked him, "Do you know why he hasn't called?"

Again he made excuses for Patrick and said that he wasn't really talking with anyone at this point. That he was going back to work soon. That he was focusing on being well enough to start within a week.

What! Was he joking? After only six weeks?

I began to get really upset. If Patrick could start work then he could make a damn phone call to me. I decided not to wait for his call and called him. I left him a detailed message. It was sweet and loving but also to the point. I wanted to know why I hadn't heard from him and when he planned on calling so I could understand what was happening. Within a few minutes Patrick called me back. I felt relieved and a little scared too. I just couldn't imagine what had occurred to have him not call. "H-How are you?" he stammered.

"How am I? You're joking, right? I have been so worried and concerned about you, like I have never been before for anyone in my life. Have you received all of my calls and emails?"

"Yes, I have and I'm sorry."

I was trying not to get too emotional during our first conversation since his surgery. But I was ready for some answers. "What's going on with you, Patrick? How's your heart? How's your leg? Can you walk now? I heard you're going to start working in a week. Is that true?" I felt like a machine gun firing all of these questions at him.

"Yes, I am going to start work in a week. The arteries are fixed in my heart. My leg is where I have the most pain still."

"What's going on with you? Why haven't you called or been in contact?"

"The first four weeks I was too sick. Then after I started feeling better and getting off so many medications, I remembered something you said to me that really made an impact."

I couldn't even imagine what it was that I could have said that would make him not want to call me.

"Okay . . . What in the world did I say?"

"You told me that you couldn't get close to a smoker. I thought you didn't want me."

"Are you serious? Of course I want you! Are you still smoking after your surgery? I thought you were going to stop."

"I did stop for a few weeks, and I am still smoking but much less than before."

"I am sorry that you could ever think that I didn't want you because of me saying that. Do you think I would have called you every day and kept in close contact with your best friend if I didn't want you? Come on, Patrick, are you serious?"

For someone who could do as much as he did in his healings, I was completely stunned to hear this coming out of his mouth. That this totally confident man could actually be feeling insecure. I didn't know what to think. I just wanted to reassure him that I did want him.

"It's not over?" he questioned.

"What? You're freaking me out, Patrick. I never once thought is was over. I thought you were too sick at first, which you were. Then I didn't have a clue what was going on with you."

"It's not over. It's not over," he kept repeating.

"No, it's not over."

"I really thought it was over and that you didn't want me."

"Are you still on a lot of medication?" I asked.

"Yes some, but not very much."

"I'm getting a little concerned that you keep repeating yourself."

"I'm sorry. I love you. I want to be with you. I want to see you soon." Now that was the guy I had been waiting to hear from.

"I'm sorry, too, that I ever said that. I love you and want to be with you too. Let's plan our next trip."

"I am going to be working next week and straight through my birthday." His birthday was May 18.

"Well, I am going to Vegas the first week of June," I said. "What are you doing?"

"I'll actually be working in Vegas that week," he said.

Finally we were going to get some much needed time together.

"I can hardly wait to see you," he said. "You're in big trouble when I see you."

"No, you're the one in trouble, mister. Are you healthy enough to have some fun?"

"Oh yes I am. Healthy enough to have a lot of fun with you."

I could feel him smiling through the phone. I was too.

"Please promise me that you will never withhold anything like this from me again. I promise to never say anything that I don't mean again to you. I'm really sorry that you had all of this on your mind when you were trying to heal. I still don't understand why you just didn't call and ask me. You are the one who is always the communicator. What happened?"

"I wanted to talk to you. I didn't have any energy the first four weeks and I slept most of the time. Also, I have been taking a lot of medications and that didn't help. I apologize, Donza. Let's put this in the past and let go of all of this now."

"Yes, all this is in the past now. Are you sure you are feeling well enough to start working so soon?"

"Yes, I'm ready to get back to work."

"Please take it easy and not work so many long hours."

"I will," he promised. "No need for you to worry anymore. Know that I love you and can't wait to see you."

"I love you too and am excited to be seeing you in June!"

Chapter Thirty-four

Our life continued on like before. We dated long-distance. We talked on the phone and shared everything. It was better than before. I could tell he had a new appreciation for his life, for our relationship, and for his work. He still had some pain in his leg but it was getting better. We were both looking forward to be seeing each other in a few weeks.

On May 13, I received a phone call from my sister, Linda. Our father had fainted and had to be rushed to the hospital. I happened to have plans to be going to St. Louis on that coming Saturday to see my family. So when my sister called on Thursday telling me that something was very wrong with our dad, I was concerned. I told her to call me as soon as she arrived at the hospital. I wanted to talk to him if he were conscious.

Linda called two hours later from the hospital. My dad was awake and ready to talk. He said to get him out of there. He was ready to go home. My dad had just turned eighty and had been losing his memory for some time now. He had been very healthy most of his life and never seemed to get sick. He still played poker with all of his children and went to the casino every chance he could get. He had been losing weight and looked frailer each time I saw him. I told him that I would be there on Saturday and would take him to the casino if he were feeling better. He reassured me that he was fine and ready to leave the hospital. I told him to let the doctors check him out and make sure everything was okay. He agreed he would and said, "I love you, hun. You hurry and get up here."

"I love you, too, Pop."

The next day, Friday, I received a hysterical call from my sister saying that I have to come home to St. Louis today. That our dad had gone into a coma and they didn't know why. It didn't look like he would survive overnight. I was so confused. I had just talked to him less than twenty-four hours earlier and he sounded fine. Now he wasn't going to live! What the hell was going on? I started to panic. I changed my flight from Saturday to Friday at six p.m. It was almost four in the afternoon so I had to hurry.

I packed as fast as I could and then, freaking out on the way to the airport, I called Patrick. He must have been working because it went to voicemail. I didn't want to leave a hysterical message, so I texted him the news. I didn't hear back from him before I left. I arrived at the airport feeling anxious. I wondered what had happened to my dad and prayed that he would be all right. I hoped that I would make it in time if he really wasn't going to survive the night.

The flight was supposed to be less than ninety minutes, but we hit a tornado on the way there and had to circle around. The flight turned into almost four hours stuck in the plane. I lost it. I couldn't control myself. I cried so hard and thought I was going to die in a plane crash. The turbulence was horrible, like out of a disaster film. I was trembling, praying, and couldn't stop sobbing. The sweet man sitting next to me was trying to say and do anything to console me. The flight attendants were all strapped down in their seats, because the winds were blowing that plane all over the place. Complete terror took over my body. I thought I was going to pass out from sheer fear.

Why, why is this happening? Not now. Please, God, land this plane safely. I want to see my father. I kept repeating that frantic mantra in my head. This was the longest flight of my life.

Finally the plane stopped bouncing. The captain got on the speaker and announced how sorry he was for all of the turbulence and the delay. We landed safely in St. Louis after a four-hour flight. I felt like kissing the ground.

Now as I left the airport I was going to have to face another real-life drama. I was already exhausted. Patrick left a sweet message on my voicemail. I called him back. He answered and I lost it right away. I told him the whole story about my dad, the flight, the tornado, everything. Patrick was such a great support. He had me take some deep breaths to relax. He always knew the perfect words to say to calm me down. By the time I arrived at the hospital I was feeling much better.

When I walked into the ICU, my sister, Linda, and my dad's girlfriend were there waiting. I was greeted with hugs. I could feel a sense of relief from my sister that I made it in time. Our father had slipped into a coma early that morning and hadn't opened his eyes the whole day. I went to his bed and whispered in his ear, "I'm here, Pop. Open your eyes. Come on, I flew from Dallas in a tornado to see you."

Dad lifted his right hand in the air and started waving it and moaning as if he could hear everything I was saying. He couldn't speak or open his eyes, but he knew I was there. That was the first time he had done anything like that I was told.

I kept pleading, "Wake up, Dad. Just wake up! You can do it!"

His eyes remained closed.

The doctors found a brain tumor and a mass on his heart. He was also septic. They couldn't move him to take any more tests. It wasn't looking good for my father. We called all our family members. Dad had a DNR order (Do Not Resuscitate), so there wasn't going to be any drastic measure to save his life.

As he lay motionless in his bed with the oxygen mask covering his mouth, many memories flashed of my dad and I when I was a little girl. I was his pride and joy. He would teach us all kinds of magic—card tricks, tricks with strings, hand tricks, anything to keep us entertained. He taught us all how to play poker and many different sorts of card games. He was the greatest joke teller too. I started to realize that I had a lot more of my dad's positive traits than I ever could have imagined.

Tears filled my eyes as I rested my head on my father's chest. I was now alone in the room with him. Our relationship had come such a long way. I had healed many issues with him over the years. It was time to say anything else I needed to say that I wasn't complete with. So I did. I cried and talked to him as if he were wide awake, listening to every word. I believe he heard everything. I had a feeling he wasn't ever going to wake up again. Even though I wanted to stay positive, I had this deep knowing that he wasn't going to be okay.

By Sunday he had gotten much worse. His breathing had become labored and there was nothing else the doctors could do for him. We had a family meeting that afternoon with the doctors to decide what we should do. They didn't know how long Dad would survive on his own without oxygen. His heart was beating strong but we knew he would never want to be hooked up on any kind of respirator or artificial support system. We all agreed to take him off the oxygen. This was Sunday, May 17, 2009 at four p.m.

We called all of our friends and family so they could come

and say their good-byes. One of my brothers couldn't make it. I put the phone up to Dad's ear so my brother could say farewell to his father.

One by one people strolled in and out saying their good-byes. Everyone was very emotional but I couldn't cry. I stayed there till ten p.m. while his heart was still beating strong. The doctors were amazed. I decided to go back to my hotel to rest for a while. They said they would call when it was getting closer to the end. I wanted to be there and hold his hand when he took his last breath. He never wanted to die alone. My oldest sister and brother, Charles, couldn't be there, nor my little sister. Only my dad's girlfriend and my brother that I didn't get along with very well were going to be there.

I prayed for a miracle that night.

Chapter Thirty-five

I received that dreaded phone call Monday morning at two a.m. My father was almost ready to go. His breathing was very shallow and his heart rate had slowed way down. We needed to get there as soon as possible. I arrived forty-five minutes later and he was still alive. His girlfriend was the only one in the room with him.

Dad's jaw had dropped open all the way, as if it were a broken hinge that couldn't be fixed. I couldn't hear him breathing at all. His breath was shallow. The heart monitor kept dropping lower in numbers every few seconds. It wasn't going to be much longer. My brother was on his way. I stood beside my father, holding his right hand, talking to him and letting him know that my brother would be there soon. Within fifteen minutes he arrived. He stood on the other side, holding Dad's left hand while his girlfriend held on to his feet. We kept saying good-bye to him again and telling him how much we all loved him.

I placed my left hand on his upper chest as I still held on to his right hand. "We love you, Pop. You can let go now. Go see Mom and your grand. They are all waiting for you." I closed my eyes and started to pray for the angels to come and be with him. As he drew his last breath, I felt this tingling energy go through my left hand, down my arm and straight to my heart. There was this overwhelming feeling of peace. It was like nothing I had ever felt before in my whole life. This calmness washed over my body. There was no fear at all, just complete serenity.

I had never witnessed anyone dying before, and to be honest, I had always had this intense fear of death. There was no fear at all. No sadness or tears. Only peace was present. It was the most incredible feeling ever.

The doctor came in to check to see if Dad was breathing. He wasn't but his heart was still beating. It kept beating for eleven minutes after he stopped breathing. It was truly amazing. His heart was still strong even after his spirit was gone. Finally the heart monitor flat-lined completely and started to beep. The doctor pronounced Dad's time of death at 3:11 a.m. May 18, 2009.

My father died on Patrick's birthday.

I knew that there must be some kind of meaning to all of this. I just didn't know what. I didn't know how I was going to call Patrick on his birthday with this news.

My dad's girlfriend, my brother, and I walked out of the hospital room very quietly. No one was crying or showing any emotions. We all remained calm. My brother said he would take care of all the funeral arrangements, which I was relieved. We stood in front of the elevators and all hugged. There was nothing else we needed to say. It was a beautiful moment.

* * *

My father was a veteran in the Navy and he would be having a military burial. I had never been to a military service before. I made it through the wake without breaking down at all. I still felt that peaceful feeling from the moment of his death and wondered if I were ever going to feel emotions again.

When we arrived at the cemetery, there were sailors dressed in full uniform and a captain standing in front of the closed casket. The American flag covered the top. Then one of the uniformed men started playing "Taps" on his bugle. I lost it. Almost everyone did at that point. I couldn't stop crying. The flood gates had opened. I didn't even care.

The captain then spoke such beautiful words about my father that if the music didn't break you, his words did. It was the most beautiful service I had ever attended. My father would have been so very proud.

PART SIX
Eternal Love

Chapter Thirty-six

I finally called Patrick later that morning to wish him happy birthday and tell him about my dad. It was the hardest thing to tell him on his birthday. He was understanding and supportive. I told him I would talk to him when I returned to Dallas in a couple of days.

Patrick let me know that he was there anytime I needed him. Later that night he texted me: *I love you and have been thinking of you constantly.* I received several texts each day from him while I was in St. Louis. I needed that connection and confirmation that he was just a phone call away.

The shock of losing my dad so fast hadn't really sunk in all the way at this point, or the intense grief that I was about to experience. I held it together very well the rest of my time there. By the time I had returned to Dallas I felt numb. I needed to see Patrick, and soon. I felt that he would be the only one in my life I could turn to and receive the love and comfort that would help heal my heart. When we talked that evening, we firmed up our plans to meet in Vegas the first week in June. I wasn't feeling much like gambling or having fun. I only wanted to spend some quality time with him. But he had plans to work long hours each day. At least we would have our nights together. My schedule was to be playing in poker tournaments during the day, which I wasn't in the mood to play at all. I had won a scholarship for a two-day poker academy course and it was a big deal. After, there would be two different events I would play in. I didn't know how I was going to be able to concentrate on playing, let alone play competitive enough to win. I would need some of Patrick's healing work to get me through. Actually, I just needed to be in his arms again, feeling the closeness and connection once more. We both needed it. We could hardly wait to see each other.

* * *

When I arrived in Vegas, Patrick had already been there for two days working nonstop. For twelve hours a day. We stayed at the same hotel but I wanted my own room since he would be working out of his most of the time. This was the first time I would be seeing him since my visit to L.A. last March. Almost three months had passed.

I was still feeling sensitive and raw since my father's death. Seeing Patrick now was just what I needed to ease my sorrow and grief. So when he texted his room number, telling me that he had two hours for a break, I was thrilled! I literally ran down the hall skipping and waving my hands in the air, rejoicing inside my heart, as if I were a child. I barely knocked on the door before it flew open. There he stood looking beautiful. I leaped into his arms as he grabbed hold tight and swung me around.

"God I've missed you!" He sighed.

Before I could say anything back, we were kissing. The intensity and passion was so overwhelming that I began to cry. I collapsed in his arms and broke down. I know that it wasn't very sexy, but I couldn't control it. He kept kissing me through my tears. I kept crying through the kissing. I felt so happy and relieved to be back in his arms. His loving touch and sweet kisses allowed the tears to process through.

We didn't make love in the traditional way in those two hours. But we did make love in a deep, spiritual, and profound emotional way that penetrated both of our hearts and souls. I felt his love on a whole other level than ever before. Something had definitely opened up for him. I could feel his presence and appreciation, for our love was stronger, deeper, more connected. This feeling I had longed for from him was now finally here. My gratitude for him and everything that we had ever shared was amplified, as well. The death of my father had made such an impact that I wanted to cherish every moment I had with my beloved Patrick. He was feeling it too with all the healing that he had gone through. We were both finally on the same page when it came to our relationship.

Patrick was very tired. He looked too thin, emaciated actually. He still had his California tan and was just as gorgeous and sexy as ever. The surgery had taken a lot out of him, and I could tell that he wasn't quite back to himself yet. I personally thought that he went back to work way too soon, but I knew that once he made up his mind about something there was no one who could ever change it. I still felt worried about him. His energy was much lower than before. Mine was too because of the grieving I was going through. We both accepted each other where we were at. He never once complained about his health or let on in any way that he was suffering or in pain. Although I could see it in his face at times that he was feeling very uncomfortable. He always kept a positive attitude and showed only love and kindness while I was with him. I loved him even more if that was possible.

We had two of the most loving and intimate nights together ever. He even worked on my body for a while so I could be more focused and clear while playing poker. The work he did really worked because in my first tournament I came in fifth place out of one hundred players. I played very well in spite of all the emotional turmoil that had been going on. Patrick was proud of my accomplishments. I never had to pretend with him. I learned how to be more real and authentic just by being in his presence. I didn't hold any of my feelings back toward him, nor did he. We kept sharing, loving, and getting closer with every minute we had together. His love was exactly what I needed to help heal my grief-stricken heart. My love was what he needed to feel the security again between us. We were both finally committed to this relationship now. Our love grew more than I could have ever dreamed. We had a second chance to love now, deeper and more profound. There wasn't anything standing in our way. It was now a matter of location and how we would be working out the long-distance part. He knew I would move anywhere to be close to him.

On our last night in Vegas I wanted us to plan our next trip together. I couldn't wait so long this time to see him, nor could he. He had a very busy summer planned traveling for his work. He was going to be gone two and three weeks at a time, working in different cities. I wanted him to come to Dallas and do his incredible healing work in my city again. The earliest he could even think about it would be in September. Although, he said we could get together at the end of July or beginning of August to spend more time with each other. That seemed so far away to me. It was only the first week in June. He assured me that we would work it out.

* * *

The second day of the poker tournament didn't go very well. It was a different event and I was playing against twelve hundred people in this one. I didn't place at all and I didn't even mind. I could only think about spending time with Patrick. He would be leaving later that day and I would stay one more night without him. He had to get back to L.A. and work there for a week before he started his hectic schedule traveling.

I still thought he was doing way too much too fast. His work was in demand and he stayed booked. I knew when he started traveling I wouldn't be able to talk with him as often. I was used to it but didn't like it nonetheless. I kept looking ahead to when we would be in the same city together and spending our free time with each other.

Our two nights in Vegas helped me heal in ways that I desperately needed. Reconnecting with Patrick after he had been ill and after my father's passing had such an everlasting positive impact on my spirit. I felt like my life wasn't put on hold anymore and that our relationship was on the right track now. Better than ever before. When it came time to say good-bye to him once again, I had a different perception about it now. No more sadness. Only love, gratitude, and appreciation for our beautiful time together. We held hands as we walked down to the lobby to catch his taxi to the airport. He stopped and stared deep into my eyes. It was a look I had never seen before from him. There was so much more love pouring out of his eyes, but something felt different. I couldn't explain it. He gently held my face in his hands and starting kissing me. I was swept away. I felt this deep love from him that was really intense. Then he held me close to his chest and kept hugging and squeezing my body tight, like he didn't want to let go. I didn't want to let go either.

He whispered, "I love you so much, never forget that."

"I love you too."

We took a deep breath at the same time.

"I will call you later when I land," he said. "I'm proud of you."

I wasn't sure what exactly he was proud of me for, the poker, dealing with all that I had just gone through, or how we had handled everything in our relationship. Whatever it was, I thanked him. We said our good-byes without any of my normal emotional reactions. Maybe that's what he was proud of me for. Keeping it together when he knew what a difficult time it had been. After he drove away, I had a sad and sick feeling sink down to the bottom of my stomach. A very different feeling than I had ever felt before. I tried to ignore it and focus only on the positive. But this sadness wouldn't go away. I told myself that I must still be processing the grief from my father's death.

Chapter Thirty-seven

I returned to Dallas the next day and Patrick called just like he said he would. We went over his busy schedule again, trying to line up some dates that would work to see each other again. We just didn't know for sure yet. He would be out of town for weeks at a time doing his seminars and private sessions. We wouldn't be talking as often as I wanted. He made sure to give me all the details of his travel dates and places. We were feeling much more secure in our relationship, and it was only going to be a short time before I would be in his arms again. I was going to have to be very patient these next several weeks and trust that our love had a very powerful purpose. Weeks had gone by and he worked such long days. Each time I spoke with him he sounded completely drained and exhausted. I became concerned about his health and wondered if he were pushing himself way too much. He would never admit it if he was, but I could hear it in his voice that he sounded tired.

* * *

It was now the middle of July and Patrick was on the East Coast working for another long extended period of time. He promised that he would take some time off after this trip and we would see each other soon. I missed him badly. When we spoke I noticed that he had a slight cough.

"How are you feeling?" I asked. "That cough doesn't sound good at all."

"I'm feeling fine. Please don't worry."

"Are you still smoking?

"I have cut way back."

"Patrick, I thought you were going to stop completely after your surgery. I have a bad feeling that if you don't stop smoking you're not going to live long." I released a big sigh of frustration.

"I know your mother and best friend died because of it and you're scared. But I'm not going to die right now." I couldn't believe those words came out of his mouth. This was a man who taught about language and how it affected your subconscious mind. Also, he didn't use the word "but" in his vocabulary nor had I ever heard him say "not." He knew that our subconscious mind drops out the negatives and only hears what is left. To hear him say that was very disturbing.

Patrick said, "Donza, I love you and will call you when I'm back in Los Angeles."

"I love you too and can't wait to see you."

He blew a kiss into the phone like he had done many times before. It made me smile. I knew that I wouldn't be talking to him for almost two weeks. As I hung up I had a very heavy feeling in my chest. *I'm just missing him*, I thought to myself.

Chapter Thirty-eight

Patrick was coming back on July 25, on a Saturday. I didn't hear from him all weekend. I thought maybe he had to stay longer or that he was too exhausted to talk and needed time to rest. So I didn't call him. Monday came and went, still no word. Finally, on Tuesday, July 28, I called his cell phone and it went straight to voicemail. Unless he was traveling he never turned his cell phone off. I left him a sweet message.

The next day my dear friend Megan from Providence, Rhode Island called. She had met Patrick when he was up there working and leading a seminar. He had really helped her. I was happy that she had met him and was finally able to experience his work. I told her that I hadn't heard from him yet.

I asked, "Do you know if he's still up there or did he make it back to California?"

"I don't know, Donza." Meagan was going to a group that night where people knew Patrick. She promised to find out when or if he had left.

* * *

On Thursday morning July 30, I received a call from Megan asking what my day was like. I was very busy and wouldn't be done till the afternoon. I only had a minute to talk. "Did you hear anything last night at your group about Patrick?"

"Let's talk after you're done working because I have to go now," she said. "Call me when you're finished."

"Okay, I will."

I worked three hours and then after lunch decided to do some grocery shopping with my little sister, Lisa, who was living with me at the time. Before I arrived at the store, Megan called again. "Can you talk now?"

"Sure, just a second." I asked my sister if she would go in and do the shopping while I spoke with my friend. I pulled up in front of the Tom Thumb and let Lisa out. Then I parked to talk with Megan.

"What's going on?" I asked.

"I want to make sure that I have your undivided attention and that you are sitting. Because my group I went to last night, Donza, the breathing class . . . it was revealed to me that it was really a lot about you. So, what I want to say to you is . . . Are you familiar with that experience where you are moved to do something and you have to give it a reason, and then it gets revealed to you later that it's not the reason at all? So I went for one reason and I'm realizing that I was divinely guided to be there. The thing I want you to know most right now is how deeply I feel for you in my heart, and I really declare that I would not be alive and walking on this planet without you. Because you got me through where the next person was. But if I hadn't had you when I did I don't know if I would have made it to that next person. Honey, I really want you to feel that."

"Megan, what the hell are you talking about? You're starting to freak me out. Are you sick?"

"I have something to share with you that is very tragic . . .

Patrick is gone."

"*What!* What are you talking about?"

"He's gone, Donza. He left. He died Tuesday morning."

"My Patrick! My Patrick! No! No! No!" I screamed. "Not my Patrick! He's not gone!"

"I'm so sorry, honey! I am so sorry. I love you so much!"

I couldn't stop screaming, "No! No! No! He's not dead! He's not dead! He didn't leave! No! Please tell me it's not true!"

"I know! I know! Scream it out, honey. Just scream it out." Megan was crying too.

"What happened? What happened?" My body was shaking. I could barely hold the phone.

"I don't know how. I don't know anything yet, Donza. I'm so sorry."

I cried into the phone. I started to feel as if the car was closing in on me. I had to get out. But my sister was still in the store shopping. Megan kept telling me to breathe. "Just breathe and to stay on the phone." The shock of it was more than I could handle.

"Stay on the phone, Donza. Don't hang up. Don't hang up."

"I have to find my sister! I have to get out of this car! I feel like I'm going to suffocate!" I opened the door. As I stepped out to put my feet on the ground, my knees buckled and I had to grab the car door to keep from collapsing. I couldn't walk. My body wouldn't stop shaking.

I sat back down in the car with the door open and buried my head in my hands, trying not to drop the phone. Megan kept talking and trying to say anything that might comfort me. At this point I couldn't hear or understand her words anymore. I was lost in a sea of emotional turmoil and pain. The news about Patrick was so intense and shocking that I didn't know how I was ever going to return to normal again. I felt like I had been shot point-blank right in the chest. I couldn't breathe. I felt this constricting feeling start to squeeze deep inside my chest, around my heart. I thought I was having a heart attack. I actually thought I was going to die.

Megan stayed on the phone and kept talking me through it. She convinced me that I could go inside the store and find my sister now. I don't know how Megan did it because I couldn't fully comprehend what all she was saying. Somehow I got out and started walking inside the store. Thank God Lisa was checking out and saw me as I walked in. She ran over right away and knew something was wrong. There was a chair against the wall. I went over and fell into the chair. I handed my sister the phone and told her, "Patrick died! Patrick died!"

I sobbed into my hands as I covered my face.

Lisa was in shock too. I heard her ask Megan, "What do I do for her?" My little sister was only nineteen. She held the bags of groceries in one hand as she tried to help me up and out of the chair to get me to the car, all while still hanging on the phone with my friend.

I drove us home but don't remember driving. I wouldn't let Lisa drive. We were only two blocks from my house and I couldn't let her drive. I couldn't talk on the phone anymore. Megan kept talking to my sister as I kept sobbing uncontrollably. I remember opening the front door to my house and going over to my sofa and collapsing onto it. That's when I really began to let go. I started screaming. "Why! Why! Why God! Why! This can't be really happening! I just lost my dad two months ago! I don't understand. Why!"

Lisa sat down as close as she could possibly be and laid her head on my torso as I lay stretched out across the couch. She tried to console me the best way she could. I still couldn't comprehend much of what she was saying. Megan told her to call my therapist and all of my closest friends and family to let them know that I needed support. I tried to talk to a few people, but by this time I was totally incoherent. The crying had now progressed into deep wailing. I just needed to be alone for a while. Lisa walked me to my bedroom and helped put my night clothes on. It was in the afternoon and she made my room as dark as a cave so that no light could get in.

I just wanted to disappear.

Somehow I thought that maybe the pain would subside if I were lying in a dark, safe place where no one could see or hear anything. Unfortunately that wasn't the case. Nothing at all could stop the emotions that kept spewing from my body. The thought that I would never see Patrick again in my lifetime was more than I could even imagine. The reality of it had not sunken in and the overwhelming shock did such a jolt to my nervous system that I felt myself going numb. As I lay in my bed curled up in a fetal position all alone in my pitch black room, I knew that my life would never be the same again.

I would never be the same.

PART SEVEN
The Healing Journey

Chapter Thirty-nine

My precious Patrick, was he really gone?

I began to remember a dream I had two days after his surgery which would have been March 18. I dreamt that he died and was in a casket and there was an old man's body lying underneath him. In my dream I looked behind the coffin and there was a hole cut out and I could see inside. It was my father, dead on the bottom of the casket and Patrick was lying dead on top of him. I remember bolting out of bed that morning and calling Kellee, one of my best friends from St. Louis, and telling her my bizarre dream. I have been known to be very intuitive in my life and have had many precognitive dreams before. This dream really terrified me because Patrick had just had surgery. My dad wasn't sick at that time.

I had called Patrick's best friend several more times that week because I was so afraid of my dream. I even told his friend that I had a really bad dream about Patrick but didn't give any details. Two months to the day my father passed away on Patrick's birthday. Then two months and ten days later, my beloved Patrick died.

What did all of this mean?

I had to find some kind of meaning to try and make sense of it all. Now wasn't the time to make sense of anything. I could only feel this intense depth of grief and pain going through me nonstop. Like a tidal wave that keeps crashing over and over against the rocks. I was feeling out of control, not knowing what to do or who to turn to. God? Turning to Him didn't seem like an option at all. I wondered what kind of a God would allow this to happen. I have always had faith and believed in a higher power, but now I questioned everything. How was I going to get through all of this loss? I didn't have any answers.

Seven hours straight of deep, core belly sobbing and wailing didn't seem to make a dent in the pain I was feeling. Lisa came into my dark bedroom several times to check in and offer food, support, anything she could think of. I appreciated her being there, even if she couldn't help. At least I knew she was there. No one could have helped me those first few days. Several friends and family members called but I didn't want to talk. These were the darkest days of my soul.

* * *

The next day I received a phone call from Patrick's home phone. I saw his name on my caller ID. My heart almost stopped. *My God, this has been just a horrible nightmare. It's all just a bad dream. He's really alive and calling me.* But when I answered the phone it was his coordinator from Los Angeles calling to let me know.

"Is it true?" I asked. "Is he really gone?"

"Yes, it's true," she said.

I started crying all over again.

"What happened? How did he die?"

"He had a heart attack between four and seven in the morning on Tuesday."

"Why didn't anyone call me?"

"We couldn't find his cell phone with all his numbers."

"I can't believe he's gone!" I sobbed. "I just can't believe it!"

"I know, I know. No one can." I could hear the sadness and disbelief in her voice as she told me that she was the one who found Patrick in the bed that morning. She had known him for thirty years and loved him too. They were like brother and sister. We were both in such shock.

"When is the funeral?" I asked.

"He didn't want a funeral or any kind of memorial."

"Are you serious? Why not?"

"He wanted to be cremated," she said in a very low tone of voice.

"Who's going to get his ashes?" I knew that he had a daughter but she lived in another state.

"His best friend and daughter will decide what to do."

"So who is taking care of everything in his apartment?"

"I am. I will wait for his daughter and we will go through all of his things together."

"Do you need any help with this?" I asked. "I will fly there to help you with anything."

"No, thank you. It's such a shock to us all. We really thought he was doing better after the surgery. He pushed himself too much."

"I know he did. I even told him to slow down. But you know he wouldn't."

"Yes, we all knew he wouldn't," she said. "It's so sad."

"It's tragic and I don't know how I'm going to get through it all."

"I know. That's how we all feel right now."

"Thank you for calling and I will call his best friend to get more details." I started getting emotional again. She cried with me. Talking with someone who was close to him and knew him for so long made me feel like I was connected to Patrick. It brought some relief.

* * *

I didn't sleep very much for days and I had to take off work for a week just to try to wrap my mind around it all and process such devastating news. I started doing this very unconventional therapy after my father died. It's called emotional transformational therapy. It helps with shock and trauma. It also balances out the right and left hemisphere of your brain to make it easier to deal with the intense feelings of grief and loss. My therapist, Susan, became my life line and one of the most invaluable people I have ever had in my life. She was such a divine inspiration and support. I went twice a week to her and I can truly say that this lady helped save my life. I thought there could be nothing worse than losing my mother. But I was wrong. Losing the love of my life and my father two months apart was way worse. There were days I didn't know how I would make it through. I started journaling a week after Patrick died. It was the best decision I ever made. Journaling brought me on this journey of healing and writing this book. I will conclude with a few passages from my journal.

* * *

August 6, 2009: One week ago I couldn't imagine that I would have been told the most devastating, tragic news that would impact my life to the core of my being. My sweet, beautiful, beloved Patrick, the love of my life, has passed away in his sleep from a heart attack. He was only in his fifties. How can this be true? The wailing that expelled from body was like no other sounds I had ever made. I never knew that I was capable of making such sounds before. Seven hours of non-stop screaming and flailing about, the total shock and complete disbelief was seeping into every cell of my body. I felt like I was being electrocuted by thousands of volts running through my veins, the pain—the unbelievable pain that had no outlet.

How do I go on? How do I get through all of this loss and grief that has left me feeling broken and alone? God, please help me understand and let there be some answers revealed soon. Let there be some peace from all of this loss and pain. My heart aches. It's more than an ache. It feels completely cracked wide open. Bleeding, oozing, out comes such deep sorrow and sadness. A depth of pain I've never known before. Is there a way through all of this? I need help. I can't do it alone. Patrick was such a special man, so important to me, the most amazing soul to ever come into my life. He's the only man who I've ever really been in love with. The only one I had been vulnerable and totally real with. The one who knew my thoughts without me ever saying a word. A true healer who loved me and accepted my many flaws. He was the light in my heart that shined so bright and pure. He was my gift from God. How can he be gone?

* * *

August 13, 2009: It's been two week since he died and my heart is broken, completely shattered. I need help picking up the pieces. The tears flow out of me like a water faucet, no end in sight for these tears. There is no closure, no memorial, no one here who knew him. So many unanswered questions. Will the pain ever subside? It feels like there is no way out of it. I feel like I'm in this deep, dark, black well. The walls are smooth. I'm alone. It feels so empty in here being this deep down. There is no light, no noise except the sounds of my intense cries. There is no ladder to climb out, nothing to hold onto or to give me hope that I will ever get out. I start to think of Patrick. I know he wouldn't want me to suffer like this.

Just feel what I feel in this moment. Remember all of the

beautiful life-altering moments we shared. I'm hanging on to every word, every memory, every smell, anything that will distract me from this unbearable pain. I begin to see a flicker of light when I look up, far in the distance. I can barely see it but I know that it's Patrick. He sends down this rope. It only reaches halfway down. I can't grab it. I don't understand. I can hardly see it but I know it's there. I'm not supposed to get out yet. It's too soon.

"Never be afraid of the pain," he says. "I'm here now and always will be. Take all the time you need. We are never separate. We are always connected forever."

I can feel his presence going through me. It doesn't feel so alone down here anymore. There is hope.

Thank you, God. Thank you, Patrick.

* * *

August 20, 2009: It's been three weeks now since I've lost my beloved. It feels like an eternity. I miss him so badly. He finally came to me in a dream last night, the first time since he died. He was wearing all white and a black jacket. He wanted to teach me more about his body language work. He was always the perpetual teacher. I listened closely to every word, and then remembered that I was dreaming and that he was gone. It felt so real. He was here visiting and saying so many things. He was ready to go. He was exhausted and in much more pain than he ever let on about.

I felt peace for a moment, calmness for the first time since his death. A knowing that I was never alone and that he would be here whenever I needed him most. I could feel him close when I breathed in deeply.

Dear God, please cradle him in your arms and let him know how much I love him and care. I miss everything about him. His touch, his lips, his passionate kisses, the soft sweet sounds of his voice, his smell, the way he knew what to say to help comfort, nurture, and help me feel better with any worries or problems I may have had. Thank you, God, for this beautiful soul who has blessed my life in so many ways. I'm grateful for his presence.

*   *   *

I become very emotional as I go back to read, write, and revisit these journal entries. Tears fill my eyes as I remember what I had to go through to get to this profound place of healing and relief. After many months of intense therapy, I allowed myself to go through the pain and many different stages of the grief process. I had learned many things. The number one thing is that I'm never alone, and that there's a spiritual path that each of us are all on. A higher power that is present even when we think we are all alone. An energy that loves us deeply and unconditionally. Even when you think it's not possible, it is present. A common thread that links us all to that one powerful source of creation. A knowingness that we are all connected in some way.

That we are all one.

Many of us have experienced profound loss, pain, and grief in our lives, but it's not the grief and all of the negative emotions that define us. It's the meaning each of us chooses to put on those feelings. Are we going to become victims and allow the pain to swallow us whole or are we going to get the lessons and learn from what has occurred? It's a process that takes you deep inside yourself to the core of your being. There were moments I wasn't sure I would make it through. There was a moment I wanted to give up, not care anymore, and not go on. But my spirit persevered. I was stronger than I ever thought possible. The sheer thought that I could someday help someone that has loved and lost gave me hope and the motivation to keep going through the healing process. I felt like there had to be a purpose for all of what I had gone through.

Writing this book and sharing my story has given me that powerful purpose and brought new life into me. I reached out for help when I just wanted to curl up in a ball and die. I allowed myself to be needy and vulnerable in front of people. To be exposed and show the rawness of my emotions. It was the hardest thing I've ever had to do. I was human and for the first time in my life I shared those parts of myself—the pain, grief, deep emotional wounds that at one time kept me feeling separate and alone. I opened up my heart and let people see into my weakened soul.

It took a lot of work, over a year, to get to place of healing my broken, grief-stricken heart. People would say to me that it's going to take time. That all you need is time. I would always get very upset when I heard those kinds of remarks. It's been almost two years now since Patrick passed and I now have a better understanding of what that means. Time does help ease the pain. When you're going through the trauma, it's not what you need to hear. I needed compassion and understanding. I needed to know that I wasn't alone. I found a support group for people who had lost their loved ones. This is one of the best things I did for myself. Taking time to grieve and allowing myself to connect with others was the greatest gift of all.

Finding the simple joys in my life again brought such healing. Trusting the process and listening to my spirit gave me a platform of knowingness that I can make a profound and positive impact on the planet. Help transform people and make a powerful difference in their lives. Showing them that they are stronger than they ever thought possible. Teaching effective ways to get through the grief and loss. Taking people on a journey of self discovery. Helping them remember that they are loved, and giving them the nurturing they desperately need during this time of healing and letting go. All that has happened in my life these past two years—all the trials and tribulations, love and losses—has not been in vain. I have overcome so much and healed my heart on the deepest levels possible.

The dark nights of my soul are over. And a new dawn brightens my life. It's now time for love again. Patrick will always be in my heart, a part of my soul. And now it's time to love again and to receive love once again. I am ready with arms wide open.

Epilogue

My final journal entry, May 22, 2011: The past races, actually blazes across my mind of a time when I felt that love was so very present, almost tangible, palpable. That I could once again be in its presence with another soul. My walls effortlessly start to tumble down and I allow my heart to be exposed for the first time in a long while. There are no boundaries or limitations in this place, just the purity of its own strength and power. Its light shines deep into my radiant soul and waits for the arrival of my new beloved. I am born into my true self . . . love. Like tiny silver sparkles lighting up my heart.

A feeling that will stay with me . . . forever.

www.ingramcontent.com/pod-product-compliance
Lightning Source LLC
La Vergne TN
LVHW011220080426
835509LV00005B/229